W9-AYF-469

Uncle John's
INDISPENSABLE
GUIDE TO
THE YEAR
2000

The 2000 Group

Bathroom Reader's Press
Ashland, Oregon

For information, write
The Bathroom Reader's Press
P.O. Box 1117
Ashland, OR 97520
www.unclejohn.com

Cover Design by Jeffery Jones,
Ashland, Oregon
Illustrations by Don Thomas,
Medford, Oregon

A special thanks to our chief researcher,
Eric Lefcowitz, for his original idea

ISBN: 1-879682-70-2

Printed in the United States of America
First printing 1998
Second printing 1999

ACKNOWLEDGMENTS

*Uncle John and the Bathroom Reader's Press
sincerely thank the people whose advice
and assistance made this book possible.*

John Javna
Jeff Altemus
Eric Lefcowitz
John Dollison
Jennifer & Sage
Adam Silver
Dee Smith
Peter McCracken
Don Thomas
Rich Stim
Sharilyn Hovind
Michael Brunsfeld
Ask Janis Editorial
Bob Weibel
Shawn Davis
Jesse & Sophie
Lisa & Larry Cooper
William Davis
Peter Workman
Janet Harris
Linda McCarthy

Antares Multimedia
Peter Stearns
Erik Linden
Andrea Freewater
Plazm Media
Gordon Javna
Lenna Lebovich
Ben Brand
Andy Wyrobik
Jack Mingo
Alan Reder
Paul Stanley
Lonnie Kirk
Julie Roeming
Bennie Slomski
Carl Jackson
Allison Waters
Steven Jensen
Bruce Harris
Paul Garnarello
Wayne Kirn

CONTENTS

INTRODUCTION

2000 is more than just a date. It's a powerful symbol. To some people it means the end of the world; to others it's the "dawning" of a New Age...

• To some people it's an invitation to the world's biggest party; to others it's a time for reflection...

• To some, 2000 is just a number—a non-event. They say it has no intrinsic meaning; it's just an arbitrary line drawn in time. And actually, they're right—it is. But that doesn't diminish it.

For centuries, the year 2000 has inspired people to examine our place in the universe. It has been a sort of deadline by which people imagined we'd know the important answers about ourselves and our nature. How far will we take science? Can it make us happy? Will we always have war? What's for breakfast?

More predictions have been made about the year 2000 than any other time in history. Frankly, it doesn't seem as though people have thought too far past it.

But now we're there...or it's here, and it's going to have an impact on our lives. We have a chance to use it as a catalyst to learn more about ourselves. Or we can just dive into the media hype...maybe get really panicky for awhile...even try to ignore the whole thing.

This book is designed to help you get the most out of 2000. We've filled it with history, anecdotes, bits of information and quotes to help you orient yourself to the Big Event—so you know what you're looking at when the millennial parade passes by.

For example: We've included interesting information on celebrations around the world, because 2000 is a global party...but we've also included material on the International Meridian Conference of 1884, which ultimately made the whole event possible.

Another example: Everyone talks about 2000 as if it has always been a part of people's lives. Actually, it was invented about 1,500 years ago by a guy named Dennis the Short. His story is fascinating; we guarantee it will change the way you look at the date.

Like Uncle John's other books, the *Indispensable Guide* is meant to be read a little at a time, starting anywhere you want. There are weighty pieces and light ones; long and short ones. It's intentionally fun and easy to read. But don't let the informality fool you—we have a serious purpose: to remind you that 2000 is an important moment in human history...and you're a part of it.

Keep It In Perspective
IT ISN'T 2000
FOR EVERYONE

*Is 2000 is the end of the world?…The beginning of
the New Age?…No big deal? We've all got an opinion,
but for much of the world the question is irrelevant—
because according to their calendars, it's not 2000…*

…It's 5760
Who Says? The Hebrew (Jewish) calendar. Their year 2000 occurred in 1760 B.C.

Origin: It's a lunar calendar that dates to 3760 B.C.—according to Jewish tradition, the date the world began.

…It's 4698
Who says? The Chinese calendar. Their year 2000 occurred in 698 B.C.

Origin: A lunar calendar dating from 2600 B.C., when the Emperor Huang Ti introduced the first cycle of the zodiac. Begins at the second new moon after the winter solstice.

…It's 1921
Who Says? The Reformed Indian Calendar. Their year 2000 will arrive in 2079 A.D.

Origin: India gained independence from England in

1947. In 1957, it officially adopted this calendar, based on the beginning of the Saka Era (a Hindu time cycle).

...It's 1421
Who Says? The Muslim Calendar. Their 2000 will arrive in 2579 A.D.
Origin: A lunar calendar that dates back to 622 A.D., the year Muhammed and his followers migrated from Mecca to Medina to avoid persecution.

...It's 1378
Who Says? The Persian calendar. Their year 2000 arrives in 2622 A.D.
Origin: This solar calendar was created by the poet and mathematician, Omar Khayyam. Iranians and many Central Asians

celebrate their new year every spring equinox.

...It's 2543
Who Says? The Thereveda Buddhist calendar. Their year 2000 occurred in 1457 A.D.
Origin: Dates from 544 B.C., the commonly accepted date of Buddha's death (he was 80). Thereveda Buddhists celebrate the new year in mid-April.

...It's 157
Who Says? The Baha'i Era calendar. Their year 2000 won't arrive until 3843 A.D.
Origin: Dates from 1844 A.D., the year the Bab (the Baha'i faith's founder) announced he was the "herald of a new religion."

The Perfect Metaphor?
THE COSMIC ODOMETER

How would you describe the approach of 2000—A giant clock ticking? A Frankenstein monster lumbering toward us? The "Great Unknown"? Here's our choice.

B ACKGROUND In 1989, Rushworth Kidder, a reporter with the *Christian Science Monitor*, called 2000 "the great cosmic odometer." Now everyone's using his idea (even us, at the top of the page)—for example:

The *Los Angeles Times*: "[The year 2000] promises to be a lot like watching all the zeroes click on the odometer of your father's Buick, but more life-altering."

The *Millennial Prophecy Report* newsletter: "It's like when the odometer ticks over in your car....[but] on a global scale. I talked to one guy who videotaped his car turning over to 100,000 miles. If it's that important when your car does it, imagine what it's like for the planet....It's gotta have meaning, right?"

The *New York Times*: "The significance of Jan. 1, 2000 is no more than the rolling over of the digits of an arbitrary odometer of time, and why not just celebrate that?"

The *Denver Post*: "The world's odometer is rolling toward the year 2000, and when those three zeroes register, big changes are coming. Then again, maybe not."

Trivia 2000
MILLENNIANA

*Here's some useless information to
impress your friends with.*

A DAY TO FORGET: Mark David Chapman—the man who shot John Lennon—will be up for parole on December 4, 2000.

WHO'S BETTING? According to a report in the London *Sunday Telegraph*, bookmaker William Hill's odds that the Second Coming of Christ will occur to mark the millennium are 1000 to 1.

BEHIND THE TIMES? 20th Century Fox has decided that by 2000, its name will become simply Fox. (Stay tuned, though—it *has* trademarked "21st Century Fox.")

LUCKY DAY: The Friday the 13th Club, based in Philadelphia, plans to disband on Friday, October 13, 2000. The club—which flaunts superstition by walking under ladders, breaking mirrors, spilling salt, and engaging in other activities to tempt fate—was formed in 1936. Its charter stipulates that the last meeting should be held in 2000. Current members plan to honor the founders' wishes and "go out with a bang."

Predictions from the Past
DINNER AT THE 2000 CAFÉ

Burgers and fries? Pizza? Not in this joint. Even 20 years ago, experts figured that by now we'd be asking waiters to bring us…

A BOTTLE OF FOOD PILLS
"By the year 2000, chemistry will replace agriculture. In the next century the day will come when everybody will carry his little gaseous tablets, his little ball of fatty matter, his little bit of sugar, his little bottle of aromatic spice, according to his personal taste."

—M. Berthelot, *Strand*
magazine, February 1901

"The businessman in 1999 [will take] a soup-pill or a concentrated meat-pill for his noon day lunch. His fair secretary [will] enjoy her office lunch in the same manner. Ice-cream pills [will be] very popular."

—Arthur Bird,
Looking Forward, (1903)

A SIDE ORDER OF UNDERWEAR

"By 2000, sawdust and wood pulp [will be] converted into sugary foods. Discarded paper table 'linen' and rayon underwear will be bought by chemical factories and converted into candy."

—John Smith,
Science Digest magazine, 1967

A WORMS & TOFU PLATTER

"It's New Year's Day in the year 2001—the beginning of the 21st century. Claire and Sara are preparing a gala brunch. On tables in the living room are bowls of buffalo gourd seeds and cottonseed 'nuts' for guests to munch on. In the refrigerator, tofu pudding is chilling...

"Squid stew is bubbling on the stove...Sara is fixing scrambled egg substitute—special for guests who long for the foods mom used to make. But she's adding a modern touch—sautéed winged bean flowers.

"Meanwhile, Claire nibbles a few fried meal worms (her favorite snacks) and rolls up the last of the Bee Won Ton. Just as she finishes, the doorbell rings. Happy New Year, everyone!"

—Paula Taylor, *The Kids'
Whole Future Catalog*, 1982

New Year's Eve, 1999
THE BIG EVENTS

*Looking for a really big New Year's Eve party?
You won't find any bigger than these.*

PARTY 2000

Location: 4,500 acres in Southern California

Event: Billed as "the Biggest Concert, Party and New Year's Eve Celebration ever held on Planet Earth." It will run for three days, starting on December 30, 1999 and continuing through the turn of the millennium. Nonstop musical entertainment is planned. Other activities will include the "world's largest cook-out" with 4,000 cement barbecues, jam sessions that any musician can join, and an indoor complex for a "comedian's showcase," a "battle of the bands," dancing, and dining.

Comment: The producer expects 2.5 million people to show up. "We want everyone who attends to have the time of their lives," he says.

For More Info: www.party2000.com

THE WORLD MILLENNIUM CELEBRATION

Location: The Great Pyramid of Cheops in Egypt, linked via satellite to the Great Wall of China, the Taj Majal in India, the Acropolis in Athens, the Eiffel Tower in Paris, and Moscow's Red Square.

Event: A 24-hour series of cultural and musical events, which will be simultaneously broadcast, time zone by time zone. The sponsor—the Millennium Society—has been gearing up for the event by hosting Countdown 2000 New Year's Eve Celebrations in locations throughout the world.

Comment: Portions of the proceeds from the celebrations will go to a scholarship fund called the Millennium Scholarship Program.

For More Info: www.millenniumsociety.org/

THE BILLENNIUM: "THE OFFICIAL CELEBRATION OF THE YEAR 2000"

Location: One place in each time zone. Possible sites: Stonehenge, the Eiffel Tower, the Mall in Washington, D.C., the Great Wall of China, Sydney Opera House (nothing confirmed as of this printing).

Event: Will take take place over a three-day period starting December 30, 1999.

Comment: Its founder calls it "a global celebration of the past, present and future in culture, education and entertainment created by and for people and communities all around the world to celebrate the Year 2000."

For More Info: www.billennium.com/home-frame.htm

What Are We Celebrating?
IT ISN'T REALLY 2000 A.D.!

*Here's a surprising bit of information: The year 2000
isn't actually the 2000th anniversary of anything.
It's based on a date someone picked out of thin air.*

T he year 2000 A.D. is supposed to be Jesus' 2000th
birthday (A.D. stands for *Anno Domini*—Latin
for "in the year of our Lord."). That's why we call
it 2000.

But it's not.

Biblical scholars have long acknowledged that December 25, 1 A.D. is just a *symbolic* representation of Jesus'
birth. As Gail and Dan Collins put it in *The Millennium
Book*:

> Let's get the big issue straight: the year 2000 is
> not the two thousandth birthday of Jesus Christ.
> He was probably born somewhere around 6 B.C.
> We know this because the New Testament is very
> clear about King Herod being the ruler of Judea at
> the time, and Herod died in 4 B.C. Case closed.

Some scholars have estimated that Jesus' birth was as
early as 20 B.C. But regardless of the exact date, the con-

sensus is that the actual "year 2000"—Jesus' 2000th birth-day—has already come and gone. (See page 2014 for an explanation.)

THE MEANING OF THE MILLENNIUM

Like most of the paradoxes associated with the millennium, the fact that our 2000 isn't the *real* 2000 doesn't seem to bother anyone.

In fact, many people think it's good news. The Collinses, for example, insist that since it isn't really the 2000th anniversary of Jesus' birth, "the calendar now belongs to far more than the Christian world." They point out that many non-Christians have started referring to the Big Date as 2000 C.E., or "Common Era," as opposed to 2000 A.D.

Even scholars who've devoted their lives to proving that 2000 isn't really 2000 are going to celebrate the Big Event. A case in point: astronomer David Hughes.

THE HUGHES STORY

In the late 1970s, David Hughes began a quest to find the actual date Jesus was born. He based his effort on the story of the three wise men who, according to biblical accounts, set out to find the baby Jesus after the star of Bethlehem appeared in the sky.

Hughes was looking for a record of astronomical conditions that would have duplicated the star's glow. And he found it: ancient Babylonian and Chinese texts revealed an extremely rare conjunction of Jupiter and Saturn that occurred in the constellation of Pisces in 7 B.C.

In 1979, Hughes published a book based on his theory: *Star of Bethlehem: An Astronomer's Confirmation.* He said he was "90% certain" that the date of Jesus' birth was September 15, 7 B.C.

Another astronomer, Percy Seymour, independently tested the theory at a planetarium in Plymouth, England. He recreated the night sky of Bethlehem based on Hughes's calculations...and a huge star appeared on the planetarium screen.

WE'LL ALL CELEBRATE ANYWAY

It is difficult to ignore the profound implications of Hughes's theory. If it's true, then the *real* year 2000 would've started on September 22, 1992.

But according to news accounts, Hughes wasn't suggesting we change anything for accuracy's sake. When asked whether he'd consider celebrating Christmas on September 15 (and moving the calendar ahead eight years), he dismissed the notion. Our conclusion: It's tradition, not accuracy, that matters most.

A Prediction from 1903
"IN 1999, ELECTRICITY WILL BE KING!"

For us, it's no big deal to flick on a light…turn up the heat…pop a burrito in the microwave. But 100 years ago, electricity was still a novelty. People could only imagine how we'd be using it in the year 2000. This excerpt is from Arthur Bird's 1903 novel, Looking Forward: A Dream of the United States of America.

I n 1999, electricity, servant-king of the world, was harnessed to everything conceivable. Everything was done merely by pressing a button.

H ouses built in that period had no stairs. Every private house had its elevator. Press a button and up it went. Houses built in that period had no chimneys. All heating and every bit of the cooking was done by electricity. If you wanted heat, press a button; more heat, press two.

L ocks and keys also became relics of a past age. No one in 1999 ever locked his house. Every house was provided with an electrical outfit. Those who desired to leave the house for a few hours attached electric gongs and alarm bells.

Another peculiar method in which electricity was utilized in 1999 robbed dentistry of some of its terrors....If a tooth ached, all one had to do was to call up a dentist on the telephone and ask to be placed on the line. The "victim," in the seclusion of his (or her) back parlor, adjusted some electrical forceps and signaled to the dentist, five blocks away, to touch it off. Then the festivities commenced.

These private tooth extracting seances became very popular. No one was there to witness the agony of the victim, as in a public dental office. If he shouted loud enough to make a hole in the sky or tried to kick the plaster off the ceiling, no one was any wiser for it.

The uses of electricity in 1999 were carried to even absurd lengths. As we know, the bite of a dog may prove more terrible than that of the co-

bra; nothing is more violent than death by hydrophobia [rabies]. With electricity this scourge was effectually removed.

In 1999 dogs over one year old had their teeth removed by electricity. Their mouths were then fitted with a false set.

During dog-days, while Sirius was in the ascendant, the false teeth were removed; all canines were kept on a vegetable diet. As a result, hydrophobia disappeared.

MILLENNIANA

Electrifying Information. It's amazing how quickly electricity became an integral part of our lives. Thomas Edison perfected the lightbulb in 1878...and it was in 1885 when Westinghouse installed the first A/C system in Buffalo, New York. It served 125,000 customers.

Some Things Never Change. The earliest-known fictional reference to the year 2000 (or at least the earliest we could find) is *The Mouse-Trap Maker*, an anti-tax pamphlet by Humphrey Hourglass published in 1790. The narrator of the story looks back on Mr. Snare, "an honest manufacturer of Mouse-Traps" in the 19th-century who becomes destitute because of bureaucrats and taxes.

Millennium Vocabulary. Here's a handy word for the year 2000: *Eschatophobia*.
Definition: "Fear of the ending of all things, and the need to escape an imagined destruction."

Important Influence #1
DENNIS THE SHORT

An obscure Ukranian monk named Dionysius Exiguus ("Dennis the Short") may be the ultimate unsung hero of the year 2000.

CLAIM TO FAME: He invented the year 2000.

BACKGROUND: Until Dionysius came up with the *Anno Domini* (A.D.) system, there was no uniform way to number years. Europeans measured time from any number of benchmarks—the founding of Rome (referred to as A.U.C.—short for the Latin *ab urbe condita*, or "from the founding of the city"), the reign of Emperor Diocletian, and so on.

The New Calendar. In 1278 A.U.C. Pope John I asked Dennis, the abbot of a Roman church and a respected scholar, to come up with a new calendar based on Jesus' birthday. This was no easy task; no one knew exactly when Jesus had been born. Working from Gospel accounts, official Roman records, and astrological charts, Dennis finally settled on December 25, 753 A.U.C.

Theoretically, December 25 should have been the first day of Dennis's new calendar. But he started the year eight days later, on January 1. The religious rationale was that it was the Feast of the Circumcision—Jesus' eighth day of life. But more likely, it was because January 1 was already New Year's Day in Roman and Latin Christian calendars.

Dennis called his first year 1 A.D. (see page 2035). That made the current year 525 A.D.

IMPACT THEN: The initial response to Dennis's calculations was silence. No one used the new system for centuries. In fact, even *he* didn't follow his own chronology (he continued to use the A.U.C system).

Using the system. Amazingly, it turns out that it took more than 1,000 years for many countries to accept the A.D. system (called *incarnation dating*).

It was officially adopted by the Church at the Synod of Whitby in 664. But no one actually *used* it until late in the eighth century, when a celebrated English historian known as "the Venerable Bede" annotated the margins of a book with A.D. dating. This work was widely copied and is probably responsible for spreading knowledge of the system around Europe.

• A.D. dating was made "universal" at the Synod of Chelsea in 816 A.D., but it still wasn't widely used by many Catholic countries until the 12th century—and even later for other nations. Britain, for example, didn't adopt the Gregorian calendar until 1752; China accepted it for civil use in 1911.

IMPACT NOW. Hardly anyone today has heard of Dennis, although his Common Calendar is the international standard. In fact, the main reason he's noticed isn't because of his achievements, but because of his screw-ups.

Dennis made two fundamental mistakes: 1) he got Christ's birthday year wrong (see page 2008), and 2) he started his calendar with 1 A.D. instead of zero (see page 2035).

Why did he do it?

It's easy to understand why Dennis got Jesus' birthday wrong—after all, he didn't have much to go on. No reference books, no computer searches.

But starting time with the year 1 goes against common sense. Logic dictates that we count a child's first birthday after a full year—when he or she is one year old—not when they're born.

So why did Dennis do it? Rushworth Kidder of the *Christian Science Monitor* speculates that "nobody wanted to describe the first year of Christianity as a zero." But Stephen Jay Gould says the answer is much simpler: "Western mathematics in the sixth century had not yet developed a concept of zero."

In other words, says futurist Jeff Altemus, "Dennis didn't really have any choice. He was a prisoner of history, like the rest of us."

Uncle John's
CELEBRITY PSYCHIC HOTLINE

Want to know what's going to happen in 2000? Don't ask us—call these celebrity psychics. Of course, they're dead…But hey, they're psychics—they'll answer.

JEANNE DIXON (1918–1996)

Claim to Fame: Supposedly predicted both John and Robert Kennedy's assassinations. In 1965, her biography, *A Gift of Prophesy*, was a bestseller. From then on she was the most famous psychic in America and the darling of tabloids like the *National Enquirer*.

Psychic Visions for 2000: Look out—the anti-Christ is "alive today in the Middle East," and will start World War III in 1999 or 2000. "He will be a military figure beyond anything the world has previously seen," Dixon wrote. "He will conquer the earth and hold it in complete mastery with the most modern weapons." There will be terrible times, but he'll be defeated when Christ returns.

Believability Factor: It's up to you—but remember, she also predicted that the South Vietnamese would win, we'd have a woman president in the '80s, and O. J. Simpson would be convicted. She once wrote a column saying

Jackie Kennedy would never remarry. It went to press as Jackie's marriage to Aristotle Onassis was announced.

EDGAR CAYCE (1877–1945)

Claim to Fame: Called "the Sleeping Prophet" because he'd lay down on a couch and go into a trance before making predictions or medical diagnoses (which were often correct). He also gave "life readings," telling people about their previous lives in Rome, Syria, Atlantis, etc. There are dozens of books on Cayce and his prophesies and a foundation carrying on his work in Virginia Beach.

Psychic Visions for 2000: Nature will go on the rampage. The poles will shift, causing earthquakes that wipe out cities all over the world. "What is the coastline now of many a land will be the bed of the ocean." (New York, Los Angeles and San Francisco are goners.) The quakes will also destroy part of the Midwest, after which the Great Lakes will flow directly into the Gulf of Mexico. Safe places include Virginia Beach (Cayce's home), parts of the Midwest, and southern and eastern Canada.

Believability Factor: Cayce made some impressive predictions—including the discovery of the Dead Sea Scrolls and the 1929 stock market crash. On the other hand, he apparently predicted some of these cataclysmic events for 1998, not 2000. But who knows—as one critic suggests, "If he knew some aspects of the future, he *could* know others."

The Chinese Calendar Says...
2000 IS THE YEAR OF THE DRAGON

Nervous about the year 2000? Here's comforting news: The Chinese calendar predicts we'll keep right on going. It's the year of the Dragon—an exciting time...but not a dangerous one.

WHY A DRAGON?

The Western calendar is linear—we're always moving forward. But the Chinese have a different conception of time; their calendar is cyclical. It is based on a 60-year cycle...which is divided into five smaller cycles. Each cycle lasts for 12 years, and each year is represented by an animal.

According to Chinese legend: "All the animals of the world were invited to come and visit Buddha. Only 12 came. To reward these animals for their loyalty, Buddha named a year for each one, in the order they appeared before him."

Thus, 1999 A.D. is the Year of the Rabbit—supposedly a relatively calm period (despite Nostradamus's prediction). But

2000 A.D. is the Year of the Dragon (the only mythological animal in the Chinese zodiac), which is a symbol of wisdom and power. It should be an interesting year—a time of action and tumult.

DRAGON PEOPLE

Were you born in a dragon year? (e.g. 1940, 1952, 1964, 1976, 1988) Many Chinese believe they take on the characteristics of the animal associated with their birth-year. "This is the animal that hides in your heart," they say. You might be interested to know that dragon people are popular, "full of vitality and enthusiasm—intelligent, gifted perfectionists." They supposedly make good artists, priests, and politicians.

On the other hand: "Dragon-people are unduly demanding on others." They have a reputation for "being foolhardy big-mouths." Fathers are said to have a difficult time giving their dragon-daughters away in marriage. And, according to zodiac lore, "dragon-women are known to go through many husbands."

Oh, Baby: It's considered good luck to have a "dragon baby." So in China, a different kind of "millennium madness" may prevail in 1999—a last-minute rush on baby-making, timed to coincide with the arrival of the Dragon.

For More Info: found.cs.nyu.edu/liaos/dragon.html

Future Flop
PAN AM'S "FIRST MOON FLIGHTS CLUB"

*In the late 1960s, Pan American World Airways
ambitiously began taking reservations for a commercial
moon flight departing in 2000. Unfortunately, they didn't
make it. There's no moon flight...and no Pan Am.*

BRIGHT IDEA
On December 21, 1968, the crew of
Apollo 8—Frank Borman, James Lovell,
Jr. and Williams Anders—lifted off from
Cape Kennedy. Their flight was covered extensively on TV, and the world was captivated by the
spectacular images of space they beamed back.

During one of Apollo 8's transmission blackouts, two
executives at Pan Am (then one of America's premier airlines) decided on a whim to call ABC-TV. They announced that the airline was now accepting reservations
for flights to the moon—which would begin by the year
2000.

SURPRISE SUCCESS
The next day *The New York Times* reported that Pan Am

had been deluged by inquiries. What began as a practical joke quickly turned into a publicity bonanza. Pan Am established the "First Moon Flights Club" and began sending out reservation confirmations.

Unbelievably, when Pan Am began running TV and radio ads with the tag line "Who ever heard of an airline with a waiting list for the moon?" TWA announced they would accept reservations, too.

ENDLESS POSSIBILITIES

If all this seems a little outrageous today, remember that during the heyday of the Apollo flights, it seemed that *anything* could happen.

"During those exciting months, the concept of scheduled passenger service to the moon quickly shifted from science fiction to the realm of the possible," a former Pan Am executive recalls.

DETAILS, DETAILS

In 1969, one Pan Am official estimated the cost of a round-trip ticket to the moon—based on 6 cents a mile—at $28,000. "It will be the longest and most expensive commercial airline flight in history," reported The *New York Times*. "But the first flight to the moon will also be the most in demand."

Membership cards for the First Moon Flights Club were

issued to residents of every state and citizens of more than 90 countries. "The amazing thing you find," one official told the *Times*, "is that most of these people are very serious about the whole idea."

ENOUGH, ALREADY

By 1971, more than 30,000 people (including future president Ronald Reagan) had signed up. That's when Pan Am decided to suspend reservations.

Membership cards are a collector's item today, and Pan Am is just a memory. In the 1980s, the company declared bankruptcy. Then in 1997, entrepreneurs bought the name and began operating a *new* airline as Pan Am; in 1998, they declared bankruptcy, too. A few months later, the name was transferred again...to a railroad. They have no moon flights planned.

*   *   *

The strangest "millennium ad" we've encountered:

Pequa Septic (a drain cleaner) ran an ad in 1995 that said: "With only five years left until the end of the millennium, there is no reason to have your drain clogged."
Huh?

2023

RANDOM THOUGHTS...

A Patriotic Effort
"America must do more than the minimum on the millennium…I believe it should be celebrated with all the grandiosity, excess and overkill that we can muster. Our national pride is at stake. There is much planning to do. Why, just the logistics of recruiting and training enough Elvis impersonators boggles the mind. We'll need the greatest procession of tall ships ever. I propose manning them with short sailors, to make them seem even taller."

—Lewis Grossberger,
New York Times, Aug. 14, 1989

It's Our Party
"Time has no divisions to mark its passage. There is never a thundersorm or blare of trumpets to announce the beginning of a new month or year. Even when a new century begins, it is only we mortals who ring bells and fire off pistols."

—Thomas Mann,
The Magic Kingdom

Post-Millennium Depression
"Someday soon, when the last millennial cookie has been

eaten and the last deadline for the end of the world has passed uneventfully, we're going to wake up and find ourselves embarked on the 21st century, third millennium of the Common Calendar. It might not be so easy to handle. ...The odds are we'll see a sort of calendrical postpartum depression.

"After all, we were born in the 1900s. We're used to standing at the end of an era, looking backward...Now the curtain's going up on a whole new show, and we can only be around for the tiniest slice of the opening act."

—Gail and Dan Collins,
The Millennium Book

In 2000...
"Authors of self-help books will be required to provide proof that they have actually helped themselves."

—Jane Wagner,
Ms. magazine, 1990

Electro-Sex
"Men of the year 2000 could enjoy exotic extras like orgasmic earlobes, replaceable sex organs, electronic aphrodisiacs, ultrasensory intercourse, and a range of ecstasy options that would make current notions of kinkiness look sedate by comparison."

—Howard Rheingold,
Excursions to the Far side of the Mind (1988)

15 Minutes of Fame
ACCIDENTAL CELEBRITIES OF 2000

Woody Allen once said that "90% of life is just showing up." That's why Uncle John predicts these people will become celebrities in 2000.

FIRST BABIES OF 2000

"On January 1, 2000, at least 24 children will claim to be the first-born of 2000—one in each time zone," notes millennium enthusiast Eric Lefcowitz.

Of the 24 lucky children, none will be luckier than the one born in the first time zone. The next day, the legend of this special "child of 2000" will be spread across the world, with every statistic recorded for posterity.

"I predict," says Lefcowitz, "that parents hoping to have the lucky baby will create a special 'springtime of love' around April Fool's Day, 1999."

Another futurist predicts that the first moments of 2000 will witness a record number of C-sections. "The competition is going to be fierce to have a child born on January 1, 2000," he declares. "For those who can't wait, a C-section may seem like a reasonable option."

THE CLASS OF 2000

In 1982, 3.5 million babies were born into the Class of 2000. They immediately attracted attention as a symbol of the new millennium. For example:

> This September, the high school class of 2000 will enter first grade. These six-year-olds will be [the first college students, workers, and voters] of the 21st century. They will be…responsible for paying off the U.S. deficit, struggling to control ozone depletion… working to limit nuclear proliferation and contending with the fluctuating world economy. Heady responsibilities for six-year-olds. (*Commonweal*, 1988)

> The Class of 2000 will be exposed to more information in one year than their grandparents encountered in their entire lives. They will have to assimilate more inventions and more new information than have appeared in the last 150 years. (Marvin Cetron and Owen Davies, *American Renaissance: Our Life at the Turn of the 21st Century*, 1989)

Now, these kids are teenagers. As graduation day approaches, they'll find themselves increasingly in the spotlight. How will they react? A preview:

> Personally, the world is going to blow up in 1999, so I don't think we're going to have any 2000,
> —Matt Butwell, Westside High School

ANYONE WHO HITS 100 IN 2000

During the last century, average life expectancy at birth in the U.S. increased by 30 years. This represents a greater gain than during *all* of previous human history. The result: In the year 2000, more centenarians will be alive than at any time in history.

Anyone who hits 100 in 2000 will make headlines for living through an entire century. And anyone over 100 will be saluted for living in three different centuries—(the 19th, the 20th, and the 21st).

There'll be plenty of qualifiers. According to projections from the National Bureau for Health Statistics, more than 72,000 people will celebrate their 100th birthday in 2000.

*   *   *

RANDOM THOUGHTS

• "Everyone has some wish in their life. I'd like to live to the year 2000. And then I'd like to be shot by a jealous husband." —**Aaron Birnbaum, noted artist, to the *New York Times* after he turned 100**

• "The car of 2000 looks depressingly like a car. It has wheels. It doesn't fly...It's not at all like those coffee-table car books said it would be." —**Nissan executive to the *Los Angeles Times***

The Times They Are a-Strangin'
MILLENNIUM MADNESS

*Have you wondered why people are starting to act
a little stranger? Get ready—experts say things
will get even crazier as we get closer to 2000.
Blame it all on "millennium madness."*

"People have been losing their grip throughout history," write John Kohut and Roland Sweet in their book, *Countdown to the Millennium.* "As we settle into the last decade of the century and the last century of the millennium, however, people are becoming downright loony tunes." For example:

SPACE CASE
The *Warsaw Voice* reports that a group called "Atrovis" in the Polish village of Niebo expects a handful of people to be evacuated by extraterrestrials in 1999. They believe 144,000 caucasians and 600,000 from other races will enter eternity. The men will get new 25-year-old bodies, the women will look like 20-year-olds.

MARY'S PEOPLE
The *New York Times* reports an increase in sightings of the Virgin Mary—which experts connect with the ap-

proach of 2000. In fact, there are so many sightings that a newsletter called "Mary's People" is now published.

HE'S BA-A-ACK

In Cuzco, Peru, 50,000 pilgrims a year are climbing Mount Auzangate to worship an image of Christ that is painted on a rock. The image, according to the *Daily Telegraph*, was discovered in 1780—the same year the Spanish killed the last great Inca leader, Tupac Amaru II. Reportedly, the pilgrimage has become popular because of the widespread belief that Tupac's body will re-emerge at the site in the year 2000 to liberate his people.

APOCALYPSE EVENTUALLY

In South Korea, a doomsday preacher named Lee Jangrim was sent to jail for convincing his followers (including some in the U.S.) that the apocalypse would occur at midnight on October 28, 1992. Many members sold their homes and possessions; a few even committed suicide. Many followers are still convinced. One told The *Chicago Tribune* that doomsday has only been postponed. "1999 is the end of the earth," he says. "That's for sure."

The word millennium *comes from combining the Latin terms* mille *("one thousand") &* annum *("year").*

The Name Game...
WHAT SHOULD YOU CALL IT?

*We all know that the year 2000 will be called
"two thousand." But what about '01...'02...
'03...'04...and the rest of the decade?*

QUESTION #1: *How do you pronounce the first
year of the third millennium?*

Here are four choices:
1. Two thousand and one
2. Two thousand-one
3. Twenty-oh-one
4. Twenty-one

The Kubrick Solution. Thanks to Stanley Kubrick's film
2001: A Space Odyssey, most people think of it as "two
thousand and one." That's no accident. According to
Fred Ordway, Kubrick's advisor on the film, "Stanley
asked if we should say 'two thousand and one' or 'twenty-
oh-one.' We decided that 'two thousand and one' sounded better....We often wondered...whether [the film's ti-
tle] would have an influence on the English language
when we got into the 21st century."

Dissent. *New York Times* columnist William Safire prefers "twenty-oh-one." Safire explains: "'Two thousand and one' may sound mysterious and futuristic today but by the time we get there, it will be a laborious mouth filler."

Popular Opinion. Apparently, Safire is in the minority. A poll conducted by the *Futurist* in 1993 showed that 62% favored "two thousand-one," 18% favored "two thousand and one," and only 10% favored Safire's choice of "twenty-oh-one."

QUESTION #2: *What do you call the first decade of the 21st century?*

Out of Date. At the turn of the last century, "aughts," "oughts," "oughties," "naughts," and "naughties," were popular. These are all out of use today. So in a 1992 editorial, The *New York Times* picked "oh's," which they termed "literal, logical and positive."

Safire Agreed. "Here is my...recommendation," he wrote, "Use *oh* in the name of the year, as in *twenty-oh-six*. It's shorter and easier than *two thousand and six*, and less negative. But hold off until 2009, when we're in prosperity or depression, before deciding what to call the decade." In The *Orlando Sentinel*, a critic commented: "You may assume too much. If we *do* survive to see the turn of the century, let's call the decade 'Whew.'"

Time Capsules
DO NOT OPEN
UNTIL 2000

*There are plenty of time capsules waiting to be
opened in the year 2000. For example...*

THE CHAMPAGNE CAPSULE

In 1984 the Millennium Society sealed messages
from 10 notables—including Ronald Reagan, George
Burns, Desmond Tutu, Bruce Springsteen, Peter Ueber-
roth, Richard Leakey, and Steven Spielberg—in an extra-
large champagne bottle.

It will be uncorked at the Cheops Pyramid Ball on December 31, 1999.

THE EXPO '70 CAPSULE

The most ambitious time capsule ever created was sealed
at Expo '70 in Osaka, Japan. A total of 12,098 objects are
stored in two separate vessels. Included are relics of the
atomic explosion at Hiroshima, a Panasonic micro-mini
television, mosquito repellant, Japanese and Western-
style toilets, a set of false teeth, and a silk condom. Also
included: documentary films of the Apollo 17 moon walk,

a heart transplant operation, and endangered Japanese animals and plants.

The first container is scheduled to be opened in 6790. The second, a short-term "control" capsule, will be opened in 2000 and inspected. If necessary, it will be treated with the latest preservation techniques. Then it will be reburied until the year 2100.

VIDEO TIME CAPSULE

As a part of the TV special "Whatta Year…1986," which aired in December, viewers were encouraged to help create a time capsule by calling a special 900 number and voting on the most memorable personalities of 1986. The capsule was filled with videotaped presentations to the winners and stored in New York's Museum of Broadcasting. It will be opened during the year 2000. (Stay tuned to find out who was picked.)

WAYSEE CAPSULE

The World Association for Celebrating the Year 2000 (WAYSEE), based in England, planted a 2000 time capsule in Jubilee Gardens on the South Bank of London. It should win some sort of award for weirdest contents. Included are a photograph of the Queen Mother, an ancient toothbrush, and a pamphlet entitled *The Vacuum Sewage System for Ships and Offshore Installations.*

What Are We Celebrating?
2000 ISN'T THE START OF A NEW MILLENNIUM

Surprised? Well, we don't expect you to change your party plans, but think about it: if 2000 isn't really 2000 (see page 2008), and it isn't really the beginning of the millennium...then what is it?

B EGINNINGS AND ENDINGS
According to several polls, the majority of Americans think the 21st century begins in the year 2000.

Technically, they're wrong—the new century actually starts on January 1, 2001.

Here's why: When the Roman Catholic Church created the Gregorian Calendar about 1,500 years ago (see page 2014), they started with the year 1 A.D.—not zero. So by the beginning of year 2 A.D., only one year had passed; by 10 A.D., only nine years; by 100 A.D., only ninety-nine years. Thus, by the year 2000, only 1,999 years will have passed. On December 31, 1999, we'll officially still have a year to go to make it to the second millennium.

YEAH, BUT...

Of course, a little detail like that isn't going to stop *us* from celebrating on January 1, 2000. But in the past, it did.

On December 25, 1799, for example, The *London Times* editorialized: "The present century will not terminate till January 1, 1801, unless it can be made out that 99 are 100...[The question of when the century begins] is a silly discussion, and only exposes the want of brains of those who disagree." In fact, most people did agree...and waited until 1801 to get excited.

In 1899, the issue arose again. A minority protested that 1900 was the "natural" century and 1901 the "artificial" one. On December 31, 1899 in London, an estimated 100,000 people "sang and danced" into what they believed was the new century. In New York, thousands more gathered in Battery Park.

But the vast majority on both continents waited until 1901 to celebrate the new century. In fact, according to one journalist, "Those celebrating the new century as of January 1, 1900 were looked down upon" as ignorant.

THE SECRET

Today, it seems remarkable that people had the patience to wait the extra year. How did they do it? *Washington Post* columnist Joel Aschenbach suggests that in 1900, at least, it was because they had no sense of the "cosmic odometer" (see page 2002) "It was pre-odometer," he explains. "The car had only just been invented. They hadn't had a chance to drive it around long enough to watch the odometer roll over to 100,000 miles."

2000 OR 2001?

In 1996, following tradition, England's Royal Observatory declared that 2001 was officially the first year of the new century. But this time, people ignored them. "The old guard...may pout to their heart's content," chuckled anthropologist Stephen Jay Gould, "but the world will rock and party on January 1, 2000."

THE DILEMMA

Obviously we *want* 2000 to be the beginning of the millennium...but it isn't. How do we resolve the issue? In his book *Questioning the Millennium*, Gould offers an ingenious suggestion. He writes:

"I know a...young man who [is] a prodigy in day-date calculation. (He can, instantaneously, give the day of the week for any date...past or future.)...I asked him recently whether the millennium comes in 2000 or 2001—and he responded unhesitatingly, 'In 2000. The first decade had only nine years.'

"What an elegant solution. And why not?"

News from 1901
HOW DID THEY WELCOME THE 20TH CENTURY?

WELCOME 1901

By today's standards, you could hardly call what folks did in 1901—the year most Americans celebrated the new century (see page 2035)—"partying." But to them it was pretty hot stuff.

NEW YORK

"New York City outdid herself...with a riot of colored electric fire, hung from invisible wires. In a plaza surrounded by titanic skyscrapers...a splendid chorus of human voices singing the glories of 'The Star Spangled Banner' beneath a lettered 'Welcome, 1901.'"

—*New York Herald*, January 1, 1901

CHICAGO

"Hordes of men and boys trudged along the pavement blowing horns and shouting through megaphones. Peddlers sold out their stocks of horns before the new century was born. Everywhere the New Year's greeting of friend to friend was not an exchange of sentiments, but a long blast on red kazoos."

—*Chicago Tribune*, January 1, 1901

WASHINGTON, D.C.

"Less noise than is usual...ushered in the new century. Chief of Police Sylvester issued stringent orders against the firing of guns and pistols, and a double force of police enforced the decree. It was not possible to suppress all noise, however, and the blowers of horns were not interfered with."

—*Washington Post*, January 1, 1901

SAN FRANCISCO

"'No monkey shines this year' appears to have been the order of the day issued by Police Chief Sullivan. The 1900 New Year's celebration had been characterized by indiscriminate public kissing on the part of persons who had not been properly presented to each other. Chief Sullivan, the killjoy, planted five cops at each corner of Market Street and ten along each block. It was a cold, clear, windless (and comparatively kissless) night."

—*Nation's Business*, reprinted in 1949

For More On 1901: italy.imdb.com/Sections/Years/1901/

Fact or Fiction?
WHAT REALLY HAPPENED IN 1000 A.D.? Part I

As the clock ticks down to 2000, will people begin to lose control? Will panicky crowds stampede grocery stores? Isn't that what happened in the last millennium?

THE STORY

According to popular lore, Europeans in the year 999 were even more panicked about the apocalypse than people are today. As the year ticked away, they gave away or sold their possessions, set their animals loose, left their homes, and huddled in churches to pray for salvation.

A DETAILED HISTORY

In his book *Doomsday: 1999 A.D.*, Charles Berlitz describes "the year of doom" in detail.

"As the year 999 neared its end a sort of mass hysteria took hold of Europe. All forms of activity became affected by the specter of impending doom...Men forgave each other their debts, husbands and wives confessed suspected and unsuspected infidelities to each other...poachers proclaimed their unlawful poachings to the lords of manors...

As the year rolled on toward its end, commerce dwellings were neglected and let fall into ruin...There was a wave of suicides as people sought to punish themselves in advance of Doomsday or simply could not stand the pressure of waiting for Judgement Day....

As the night of December 31 approached, the general frenzy reached new heights. In Rome, the immense Basilica of St. Peter's was crowded for the midnight mass which in the belief of many might be the last mass they would ever attend on earth.

MEANWHILE, IN ROME...

Frederick H. Martens writes in *The Story of Human Life* that there was a dramatic New Year's Eve climax at St. Peter's:

"Pope Sylvester II stood before the high altar. The church was overcrowded, all in it lay on their knees. The silence was so great that the rustling of the Pope's white sleeves as he moved about the altar could be heard. And there was still another sound...that seemed to measure out the last minutes of the earth's thousand years of existence between towns and cities was largely interrupted; since the coming of Christ—the door of the church sacristy stood open, and the audience heard the regular, uninterrupted tick, tick, tock of the great clock which hung within....

The midnight mass had been said, and a deathly silence fell. The audience waited....Pope Sylvester said not a word....The clock kept on ticking....Like children afraid of the dark, all those in the church lay with their faces to the ground, and did not venture to look up. The sweat of terror ran from many an icy brow, and knees and feet which had fallen asleep lost all feeling. Then, suddenly—the clock stopped ticking! Among the congregation the beginning of a scream of terror began to form in many a throat. Stricken dead by fear, several bodies dropped on the stone floor.

WHEW!

Berlitz picks up the narrative again: "Then the clock began to strike. It struck one, two, three, four. It struck twelve. The twelfth stroke echoed out, and a deathly silence still reigned! Then it was that Pope Sylvester turned around, and with the proud smile of a victor stretched out his hands in blessing over the heads of those who filled the church....Men and women fell in each other's arms, laughing and crying and exchanging the kiss of peace. Thus ended the thousandth year after the birth of Christ."

It's a pretty exciting story...but is any of it true?
Turn to page 2181 for Part II.

Oops!
POLITICAL
PREDICTIONS FOR 2000

*As if you need any more proof that politicians
don't know what they're talking about....*

"One can only smile at the thought of England
and the United States planning for the year
2000. They will be lucky if they survive until 1950."

—Joseph Goebbels,
Nazi propaganda minister, 1941

❖   ❖   ❖   ❖

"Capitalism [is] a museum piece....[We] will demonstrate
conclusively to 'all and everyone' how right Marx, Lenin
and their followers were in history's eyes."

—Comrade V. Kosolapov,
Mankind and the Year 2000 (1976)

❖   ❖   ❖   ❖

"I am confident that [in 2000] the Republican Party will
pick a nominee that will beat Bill Clinton."

—Dan Quayle,
Ex-vice president of the U.S., 1998

1000 A.D. and 2000 A.D.
THE AMAZING
SIMILARITIES!

Trying to compare the years 1000 and 2000 A.D. seems
ludicrous. After all, in 1000 Europeans were living in
near-primitive conditions. They hadn't even invented bath-
rooms (an important milestone to Uncle John). But the
comparison is inevitable...and in his book Apocalypse
Wow!, James Finn Garner reveals some astonishing
parallels. Could history be repeating itself?
Judge for yourself!

1000 A.D.	NOW
"Median life expectancy: 17"	"Median emotional age: 17"
"An ignorant, illiterate population relied on privileged, self-serving demagogues to interpret the world around them."	"24-hour talk radio"

1000 A.D.	NOW
"People live in rickety huts and lean-tos, constantly fearful of attack."	"People live in 10-room houses in gated communities, constantly fearful of attack."
"Vikings invade settlements, plunder populations, and destroy local European culture."	"The world is overrun by satellite TV and McDonald's."
"Traveling mountebanks, magicians, and swindlers"	"Economists, pollsters, and televangelists"

...And our chief researcher, Eric Lefcowitz, adds:

The king of England, Ethelred the Unready, was widely perceived as a weak personality, and a disgrace to his family.	Prince Charles, ditto.

Have we crashed yet?

THE COMPUTER BUG
Part 1

*As we get closer to the year 2000, you'll be hearing more
and more about the Y2K computer bug. Like many
of us, you might be wondering how such a small
thing can be such a big problem...and how it
came about in the first place.*

WHAT'S THE PROBLEM?

Variously called the Year 2000 Problem, the Millennium Bug, or Y2K, it's a glitch that keeps computers from accurately calculating dates with years after 1999.

Many older systems were designed to use only two digits to designate the year (91, for example, represents 1991). These systems assume that the first two digits of every year are 19.

The trouble starts when these systems have to handle dates beyond the 1900s. In 2000, for example, a program that tries to figure the age of a person born in 1963 will subtract 63 from 00 and get –63.

What's the big deal? Imagine the nightmare you'd go through trying to deal with a company or government agency whose computers say that you have a negative number for your age—and therefore don't exist!

HOW'D WE GET HERE?

The problem began in the 1960s. A megabyte of memory then could cost tens of thousands of dollars. So programmers chose to save money and space by taking their two-digit shortcut.

Most programmers didn't expect their systems to last into the 1990s—and for the most part, they haven't. But as new systems came into use, there was a need to make them compatible with older systems. So the convention of using two-digit numbers to represent years continued. And while at least some programmers were aware of the potential problem, they apparently figured someone in the future would take care of it.

TOWN CRIER

Unfortunately, no one did. In fact, the problem was largely unknown to the general public and virtually ignored by government officials until the late 1980s.

That changed in 1989 when Kathy Adams, assistant deputy commissioner for systems at the Social Security Administration, discovered the problem in her department.

"We had someone try to arrange a payment schedule that went into the year 2000, and when they tried to put it in, the system failed," recalls Adams. "Once programmers realized it was the inability to process the year 2000 date, we realized it had the potential to be a big problem."

She began warning other government officials, but for the next six years, she was mostly ignored. In 1995, however, she finally got through to someone.

"At a retreat one weekend, she cornered me, gave me a paper on the subject and told me all about it," says Anthony Valletta, acting Secretary of Defense. "I came running into the Pentagon on Monday and started telling some senior people and I got half of them saying, 'What are you crazy?' and I got some people saying, 'That sounds like something we ought to check into.'"

"That meeting," writes Fred Kaplan in the *Boston Globe*, "resulted in a directive sent to every relevant office in the Defense Dept. to address Y2K as a top priority."

SPARK

None of this should have been a surprise, though, according to Adams. "Everyone should have known this was going to be a problem," she says. "But in the 60s, 70s, and 80s, everyone thought this code wasn't going to be around by 2000."

Programmers were aware of it—and some had been trying to alert the public. At least one newsletter covering Y2K (called "Tick, Tick, Tick...") existed in the early '90s and a few articles had touched on the problem. But Adams' talk with Valletta finally got the ball rolling.

Soon afterward, the issue started getting more media and government attention. For example:

• Websites devoted to the issue (e.g., "The Year 2000 Information Center") began popping up all over the web.

• The U.S. Congress created subcommittes to probe the problem.

• Several newsmagazines ran cover stories on Y2K.

• The federal government started receiving progress reviews on how well they were responding to the problem.

• The New York Stock Exchange traded on the de Jager Year 2000 Index (an index which represents shares of firms working on the Y2K problem).

• August 19 was declared Global Y2K Awareness Day by computer industry leaders.

We can only assume that the closer we get to the year 2000, the more we're bound to hear about Y2K.

WHAT'S AFFECTED?

Just about anything containing a computer chip can go awry. The biggest problem is in mainframe systems, which hold more data and programs than PCs, but any system that relies on date calculations could be affected. This includes anything from weapon systems and power plants to telephones and VCRs. "Virtually every government, state and municipality," warns *Newsweek*, "as well as every large, midsize and small business in the world is going to have to deal with this." **For part 2, turn to page 2139.**

Predictions from the Past

"WE'LL ALL BE RICH AND LAZY IN 2000!"

According to experts in the 1960s, life in the year 2000 was supposed to go something like this: Get up in the morning, fix a cup of coffee, read the newspaper, watch some TV, and lay around trying to figure out what to do. Sound too good to be true? It was.

A GOLDEN AGE

"By 2000, the machines will be producing so much that everyone in the U.S. will, in effect, be independently wealthy. With government benefits, even nonworking families will have, by one estimate, an annual income of $30,000–$40,000 (in 1966 dollars). How to use leisure meaningfully will be a major problem."

—*Time*, **February 25, 1966**

THE EASY LIFE

"By the year 2000, people will work no more than four days a week and less than eight hours a day. With legal holidays and long vacations, this could result in an annual working period of 147 days and 218 days off."

—**The** *New York Times*, **October 19, 1967**

RICH RETIREMENT

"By A.D. 2000 one can retire with a comfortable income at the age of 50; and retirement will be compulsory at 60, except for those with skills in scant supply."

—R. G. Ruste, *American Heritage, Prognosis A.D. 2000*, 1967

LEISURE-TIME FUN

"The main result of all these developments will be to eliminate 99 percent of human activity, and to leave our descendants faced with a future of utter boredom, where the main problem in life is deciding which of the several hundred TV channels to select."

—Arthur C. Clarke, *The World of 2001* (1968)

HOME EXERCISE

"It's not too difficult to imagine that by the year 2000, we may have become a nation of voluntary leisure-time shut-ins, amused by a console in the living room and exercised by a vibrator in the bath."

—Editors of News Front, *The Image of the Future, 1967...2000*, (1968)

International Timekeeper
THE BIRTH OF
INTERNATIONAL TIME

When the clock strikes midnight on December 31,
1999, billions of people around the globe will cheer.
Most will have no idea that they're also celebrating the
evolution of international timekeeping over last 100
years. Here's why we can have a global party.

B ACKGROUND
One hundred twenty-five years ago, there were
more than 70 different time zones in the U.S. Every region had its own local time.

This made it difficult to conduct business on a national
scale. So in 1883, the railroad industry introduced a new
system of four time zones. "Railroad time" wasn't legally
binding, but it *was* practical—and most of the U.S. eventually adopted it.

THE MERIDIAN CONFERENCE
Internationally, the same scenario was unfolding—
shipping schedules and railroad timetables, for example,
were difficult to coordinate because every country had a
different time system (and some had several).

U.S. president Chester A. Arthur decided the rest of the world should be organized into time zones, too. So in 1884 he hosted the International Meridian Conference in Washington, D.C.

Forty-one representatives from 25 countries showed up to create a standard international time. The only problem was, they couldn't agree on which country would be the official timekeeper…or where in the world the official day would start (this spot—0° longitude—was to be called the "prime meridian").

JOCKEYING FOR POSITION

The U.S. and Britain suggested the meridian line pass through the Royal Greenwich Observatory in Greenwich, England. France insisted on a location in Paris. Others suggested starting the day in Egypt, near the pyramids.

In the end, U.S. and British diplomacy won out; the vote was 22 to 1 for Greenwich, with Brazil and France abstaining in protest. This established Greenwich Mean Time as the world standard.

Not everyone was happy with the plan, though. A number of nations, including Russia, Ireland, France, and most of South America, boycotted it. So when the 20th century arrived, it arrived at a different time in each place. Practically speaking, there was still no international time. It took a world war to change that.

THE WORLD WAR STANDARD

When World War I began, standard international time was still a shaky experiment.

"Once fighting began," says Michael O'Malley in *Keeping Time*, "coordinated standard timetables and synchronized watches kept the whole machinery of violence running as smoothly as possible. The war probably did more to establish world standard time by law than any actions of scientists or politicians."

When the war was over in 1918, most countries continued to set their clocks by Greenwich Mean Time. It was the first occasion in the history of the world that (almost) everyone was on the same time system.

And that's why we can have a global party on December 31, 1999.

For More of the Story, see page 2071.

WHY GREENWICH?

The Greenwich Observatory was built in 1675 to help sailors determine their north/south positions at sea. In 1852, an electric clock was placed at the Observatory. Eventually, English railway companies designated it as the standard for their travel schedules. Essentially, this made it the official clock of the British Empire.

Mark Your Calendar
IT'S A LEAP YEAR, TOO

Every four years, February gets a 29th day, right?
Well, no. The rules for leap years are different at
the beginning of a century. That's why February 29,
2000 will be the most notable leap day in history.

B ACKGROUND
Until 1587, Europe used a calendar created by Julius
Caesar in 45 B.C. This calendar is based on the assump-
tion that a solar year is 365 1/4 days.

Obviously, you can't have a fraction of a day on a calendar. So Caesar balanced things out by adding a 366th
day to the calendar every four years. He called these "leap
years." ***

Caesar's leap year would have been a great solution...if
a solar year really was 365 1/4 days. But it isn't. It's
365.2422 days—or 11 minutes, 14
seconds shorter.

WHERE DOES THE TIME GO?
Over the centuries, those missing
minutes added up. By the 16th century, the calendar was more than 10
days off. Farmers who wanted to plant by the vernal equi-

nox (March 21 for us) couldn't predict when it would occur...and church leaders couldn't predict Easter's date.

Finally, in 1587, Pope Gregory XIII convened a committee to stabilize the calendar. Their conclusion: They could do it by skipping a leap year every 100 years. To keep it simple, they designated the first year of each century (1700, 1800, etc.) as the leap year to skip.

Case closed? No. Further calculations showed they'd shaved *too much* time off the calendar—they had to put one leap year back. So they decided that every 400 years, when the first year of a century (the "centennial year") is divisible by four, there would be a leap year. This is called a "quad-centennial" leap year.

MAKING HISTORY

The first quad-centennial leap year was 1600. But the new calendar wasn't adopted in many countries until long after that. So the year 2000 will be the first time in history that the whole world observes a quad-centennial leap year. Enjoy it—the next one won't occur until 2400.

*** Why a "Leap" Year? Normally, if a date—say March 6, for example—falls on a Monday in one year, it will fall on Tuesday the following year. But if it's a leap year, it will skip Tuesday, and *leap* to Wednesday.

For More Info: www.ast.cam.ac.uk/RGO/leaflets/leapyear/leapyear.html

Uncle John's
HANDY GUIDE TO THE PROPHETS OF DOOM #1

You may be able to escape doom in 2000, but you can't escape people talking about it. We've created this section so you won't feel left out of the conversation. Here are a few of the famous (or is that infamous?) people who expected the worst in 2000.

OUR LADY OF FATIMA

Background: In 1917, the Virgin Mary appeared to three young children in the village of Fatima, Portugal. According to Lucia dos Santos, oldest of the three, Mary shared a secret revelation composed of three parts: 1) A graphic, frightening vision of hell; 2) World War II would occur; 3) Unknown. Lucia kept it to herself until the mid-1940s, when she wrote it down and sent it to the Vatican. It wasn't read until 1960, by Pope John XXIII. Observers say he was so shaken by the prophecy that he resealed the envelope and never revealed it.

As far as we know, it's still sealed. But texts claiming to be the third prophecy have begun appearing on the internet and in tabloids.

Doomsday 2000: Speculation is that it's an apocalyptic message involving a nuclear holocaust; mankind will suffer a great plague; Satan will rule the earth; and church officials will fight one another. A huge war will cause fire and smoke to fall from the sky and millions will die by the hour. Those who survive will envy the dead.

Believability Factor: Lucia didn't reveal the first two prophecies until 1941. And according to several sources, she has changed or embellished her story a few times. So it's just as possible the contents of the envelope are still a secret because they're not terribly interesting...except as a secret.

ST. MALACHY (1094–1148)

Background: Malachy O'Morgain was a 12th-century Irish bishop. During a visit to Jerusalem, he had a vision that led him to write down the names and descriptions of 112 men he believed would be popes from 1143 A.D. on.

Doomsday 2000: According to Malachy, the last pope on the list—Peter the Roman—will be the last pope ever. John Paul II is the 110th, but depending on how you interpret the list, there might only be one pope to go.

And that could happen at any time. Specifically, Malachy predicted:

In the final persecution of the Holy Roman Church

there will reign Peter the Roman, who will feed
his flock among many tribulations, after which the
seven-hilled city (Rome) will be destroyed and
the dreadful Judge (God) will judge the people.

Believability Factor: Malachy's predictions weren't "discovered" until 1595. Not surprisingly, descriptions of the 74 popes from 1143 to that date are remarkably accurate. The question is...what about the predictions *after* that? And the answer is...some are wrong, but some are remarkably accurate.

Is that just luck? There's no way to answer—which is why people are still paying attention. "The Malachy prophesies are intriguing," writes Kevin McClure in *The Fortean Times Book of the Millennium*. "The information is so slight, yet parts of it can seem convincing....I wouldn't dismiss it all too lightly."

MOTHER SHIPTON (1488–1561)

Background: An historic figure in northern England, reputedly as famous as Nostradamus. She was a 16th-century witch who lived in a cave. Legend has it that her mother was "impregnated by a being of awesome, superhuman origin, who rewarded her sexual generosity by giving her powers similar to his own." She passed these powers on to her daughter.

Mother Shipton has been credited with predicting the defeat of the Spanish Armada, World War II, the invention of the car, and lots more. Her predictions for 2000 were reportedly discovered in an Australian library.

Doomsday 2000: Shipton is quoted as saying that the "Son of Man" will arise from the Middle East with a fierce beast in his arms and invade France. She wrote:

> An Eagle [U.S.] shall destroy castles of the Thames, and there shall be crowned the Son of Man, and the fourth year shall be many battles for the faith and the Son of Man, with the Eagles shall be preferred, and there shall be peace over the world, and there shall be plenty of fruit, and then shall he go to the land of the Cross. [Modern interpretation: The U.S. will defeat the Arabs in a religious war lasting four years.]

Then the world will end.

Believability Factor: Mother Shipton was famous long before many of her written predictions turned up. They added to her fame—but in 1862, a British editor named Charles Hindley claimed he had written many of them himself. And there's no telling who actually created the prophecies for 2000. Nonetheless, there are believers.

Ready for more? See page 2092 for the next installment of Uncle John's Handy Guide to the Prophets of Doom.

$ *Cashing in on 2000* $
MILLENNIUM MARKETING

*"As the millennium approaches," says The Chicago
Tribune, "there will be prophets, and then there
will be profits." Here are some of the sillier ways
companies are linking their products to 2000.*

THE MILLENNIUM

What It Is: A polished, stainless steel casket from
the Batesville Casket Co.

Millennium Connection: "It has a contemporary look
and innovative design."

TOOTHBRUSH FOR THE MILLENNIUM

What It Is: A toothbrush with "twin heads and greater
contact and greater stimulation of the gums."

Millennium Connection: "It heralds a new age in what a
toothbrush can do."

PORTA-CHIAVE 2000

What It Is: A solid brass key holder, from Steamer Trunk
Merchants

Millennium Connection: "Give it to the friend you want
to see again and again in the new millennium."

MILLENNIUM VANILLA

What It Is: A vanilla extract used in ice cream, made by David Michael & Co.

Millennium Connection: The ice cream tastes so good, says a spokesman, "it's a way to celebrate the year 2000."

THE THIRD MILLENNIUM BIBLE

What It Is: The *King James Bible*—first published in 1611.

Millennium Connection: It's "a classic and unchanging Bible for the third millennium."

THE MILLENNIUM

What It Is: A semiautomatic nine-millimeter gun, from Taurus International Manufacturing

Millennium Connection: "It's futuristic."

OFFICIAL CANDY OF THE NEW MILLENNIUM

What It Is: M&Ms (which, by the way, have been around for over 50 years)

Millennium Connection: MM is 2000 in Roman numerals.

SMILEY 2000

What It Is: A product line—pins, t-shirts, etc.—featuring an updated version of the yellow smiley face from the '60s.

Millennium Connection: "With the year 2000 approaching, what's old is new and that means Smiley too!"

Important Influence #2
THE BOOK OF REVELATION

Concerned about the end of the world? Whether your major focus is on Y2K, a pole shift, or some other scenario, the chances are you've been influenced by Revelation.

CLAIM TO FAME: If apocalyptic thinking is a hallmark of the millennium, then the *Book of Revelation* is...well...its bible. *Revelation*'s terrifying imagery and foreboding warnings are a constant companion to the creeping sense of doom many people feel as 2000 approaches.

BACKGROUND: *Revelation* is the last book in the Christian Bible.

Much of its history is still unknown. Scholars estimate it was written between 65 and 100 A.D (probably around the year 90). Many believe its author was an early Christian named John, exiled by the Romans to the Greek island of Patmos for "confessing" his belief in Christianity. But there's no consensus on this. Some insist it was John the Apostle, who wrote the Gospel; others think the book had several authors.

Revelation is divided into two main parts. The first is a letter to "the seven churches of Asia"—early Christian churches located in what is now Turkey. It encourages them to hold onto their Christian faith, despite persecution and Roman demands that they worship the Emperor.

The Visions. The second section chronicles what John describes as a series of divine visions. They are filled with vivid, horrific imagery of the apocalypse. A brief summary from *The Book of Predictions*:

> The central theme of *Revelation* concerns a book which is held closed by seven seals. The breaking of each seal reveals another aspect of the apocalypse. The first four seals bring to life the famous four horsemen of the apocalypse riding a white, red, black, and an ashen-colored horse. The four horsemen personify the evils of war—Conquest, Slaughter, Famine, and Death. The broken fifth seal reveals martyrs who have been slaughtered for "the word of God." They are each given a white robe and told to rest a little longer and await the arrival of more martyrs.
>
> A violent earthquake takes place upon breaking the sixth seal...The breaking of the seventh seal is followed by silence in heaven. Seven angels then appear and are given trumpets. The sounding of each horn brings a new disaster on earth...
>
> In *Revelation* 13, a terrible beast appears. This marks the arrival of the Antichrist and deception and devastation throughout he world.

Eventually, it says, Christ will return to defeat Satan's forces and destroy evil. He will reign for 1,000 years... then Satan will be back for one last battle at Armageddon. Christ will win again; Satan and his minions will be cast into a lake of fire and brimstone, and all of the dead will be resurrected for a Last Judgment.

Of course, to get the full effect, it's best to read the *Book of Revelation* for yourself.

IMPACT THEN: "Little is known about *Revelation*'s impact in its own time," says Dr. Douglas Ottati of Union Theological Seminary in Richmond, Virginia, "but it's an example of a particular type of preaching, where God's history vindicates oppressed minorities—in this case, the Christians. It's a safe guess that it was effective, and provided solace for members of the Asian churches."

IMPACT NOW: It's one of the most influential works in western culture. Millions of people believe every word is literal truth, and live with the knowledge that sooner or later, everything described in it will come to pass (many believe sooner—perhaps 2000).

But whether you're a believer or not, you can't escape its apocalyptic message. It's in pop culture (the 1998 film *Armageddon* got its title from *Revelation*), politics (James Watt, U.S. Secretary of the Interior in the early '80s, said he didn't have to worry about environmental degradation—or do anything about it—because the "world will surely end before any deep damage is done"), common language ("four horsemen of the apocalypse," "666," "fire and brimstone"), the arts, and so on.

Birth of the Millennium. But it's even more influential than that: many experts think Western society's interest in the millennium as a unit of time evolved from a passage in the *Book of Revelation*.

Here's why: The term "millennium" was originally used in reference to the 1000-year reign of Christ described in *Revelation*. No specific date is given for it, so early scholars scoured the Bible for a clue. They found it in 2 *Peter* 3:8—"One day is with the Lord as a thousand years."

They reasoned that since God created the world in six days and rested on the seventh, the world will exist for 6,000 years (6 "days"); then Christ's millennium will begin (the 7th "day"). They calculated that the earth had existed for 4,000 years before Christ. That meant Christ would be back in 2000 A.D. to fulfill the prophecy.

Over time, the secular millennium has taken on an importance of its own. As a result, today people are focused on the calendric implications of 2000 as well as the religious ones.

What Will You Be Drinking?
THE SPIRITS OF 2000

It's almost midnight on New Year Year's Eve—time to toast the millennium. You reach into the fridge and pull out...what? Well, it's a unique occasion—maybe you want something extra-special. Here are our suggestions:

F RED THE BEER. "You've heard about Bud, the beer touted to taste best within 110 days of bottling," reported The *Wall Street Journal* in 1998. "Now meet Fred, the beer you're not even supposed to crack open until the millennium."

In November 1997, Hair of the Dog Brewing Co. in Portland, Oregon, created Fred—a beer designed to get better as it ages. The first batch sold out in an hour.

Fred contains 11.5% alcohol. "It's an acquired taste, not a six-pack kind of beer," explains a beer critic. "If you drink a six-pack of it, you'll be on the floor."

For More Info: www.hairofthedog.com/beers.htm

MILLENNIUM SCOTCH.

• In the mid-1990s, a reporter for The *Toronto Star* wrote about visiting the Bushmills distillery in County Antrim, Ireland—and seeing rows of barrels marked "Millennium" in one of the warehouses. The barrels had been filled with whiskey in 1975, to be broached in the year 2000.

• In 1992, the Aberlour Distillery offered a "perfectly aged," 10-year-old, premium, single-malt scotch whiskey to be delivered in the fall of 1999. Cost: $2,700 per bottle (it had to be paid in 1992). *USA Today* called it "the gift of the century—or at least a gift for the end of the century." Maybe someone will offer you a celebration sip at midnight.

ROEDERER CHAMPAGNE. Supply is limited because "real" champagne can only be produced in the 12,000-acre Champagne region of France. The result: Some experts are warning of a shortage. "1999 will be a record year for the industry," a beverage analyst in London has said. "There's a potential for shortages—at the top end of the scale in particular."

For big spenders, special millennium champagne will be available. In 1990, Louis Roederer Champagne announced it was bottling 2,000 methuselahs (six liters—about eight bottles' worth) of *Cristal*, its top-of-the-line product, to be released in 1999. Each will be numbered and cost $2,000.

But a book called *Vintage Timecharts: The Pedigree and Performance of Fine Wines to the Year 2000*, by Mitchell Beazley, recommends Roederer's deluxe 1983 champagne vintage. You have a better chance of finding it, too— 25,170,000 cases were produced.

For More Info On Champagne: www.moet.com/

Party Tip
THREE HOT SPOTS

*Got plans for New Year's Eve yet? If you're
feeling adventurous, Uncle John's Travel
Bureau has a few ideas for you.*

1. ARMAGEDDON

Yes, it's a real place (in Israel, southeast of Haifa)—and the
perfect tourist destination for apocalypse buffs.

In ancient times, it was a a strategic stop on the highway between Egypt and Mesopotamia and the site of many
historic battles. But today its main attraction is biblical.
According to *Revelation*, Armageddon will be the site of
the final battle at the end of time. Just think—if this cataclysmic event takes place on December 31, 1999 (and
many people believe it will), you'll
have a front-row seat.

Added bonus: Friends and
family will appreciate the
postcard marked "Armaged-
don 2000."

2. THE PANAMA CANAL

The 51-mile canal, which opened in 1914, is reportedly
the most valuable piece of real estate in the Western Hem-

isphere. It's not usually anyone's first choice for a New Year's Eve bash. But if you're Panamanian (or want to act like you are for the night), it's the place to ring in the millennium. People in Panama started planning their celebrations in 1977 when the U.S. agreed to turn over the Canal Territory to Panama on December 31, 1999. A raucous party is expected to start when the Panamanian flag is raised at noon. It will go on well into the night—and 2000.

3. NAZARETH

According to *Travel Weekly*, "The Nazareth area of the Galilee is gearing up for the celebration of the millennium. The year 2000 is expected to bring Christian pilgrims by the thousands to the sites of Jesus' ministry."

Nazareth's biggest attraction is the Church of the Annunciation, where Mary was informed she'd give birth to Jesus. Special celebrations include Feast of Annunciation (March), Feast of the Assumption (August), and, of course, Christmas (December).

Will there be room in the inn? Don't worry—the city has announced it's doubling hotel capacity by the year 2000.

International Timekeeper
WHO DECIDES WHEN 2000 STARTS?

How can you be sure it's 2000? Dick Clark or some other announcer will say so on TV. But who will tell them? Here's the scoop on earth's official timekeeper.

B ACKGROUND
The Royal Greenwich Observatory is the most famous timekeeper in the world. But although the prime meridian runs through Greenwich (see page 2052), the Observatory isn't in charge of the world's clock anymore. The Observatory isn't even in Greenwich—it's in Cambridge. In fact, it may not even exist by the time you read this—plans have been made to merge it with an observatory in Edinburgh.

So who will be relaying the message that 2000 has finally arrived? A group you've probably never even heard of.

MEET THE BIPM
The *Bureau International des Poids et Mesures* (BIPM) in Paris, France, is now the world's timekeeper. It's not a new organization—it was created in 1875 to establish an

international system of measurements. It is an inter-governmental body with an international staff.

At some point in the last few decades, they also became the official international timekeeper. What do they do? Today international time is calculated by gathering data from 230 atomic clocks maintained in 50 national timing centers (observatories or labs working in meteorology). From this, they establish something called "international atomic time" and "coordinated universal time."

We could go into additional detail, but it would take too long. If you really want to know more about timekeeping—like what's an atomic clock?—get online and check out these Web sites: tycho.usno.navy.mil/frontpage.html *or* www.bipm.fr/

For the Record: The official U.S. time is kept by the U.S Naval Observatory Master Clock in Washington, D.C.

• The U.S. Naval Observatory has been responsible for time management since 1845. The original clock was a time ball set atop a 9.6-inch telescope dome and dropped every day at noon.

• The Master Clock now is a system of dozens of separate, independently operating "cesium atomic clocks" and hydrogen master clocks maintained in environmentally sealed vaults. The atomic clocks lose only one minute every 200,000 years.

Whatever Happened to...
THE "FREEZER ERA"

*At the height of the Space Age, people seemed to
believe there was no limit to what scientists could
accomplish by 2000. Case in point: cryonics.
Just when you thought you thaw it all…*

FREEZE-WAIT-REANIMATE
In the mid-1960s, a handful of
people thought they'd found the key
to immortality. Their secret: the "science" of *cryonics* (based on the Greek
word *kryos*, "to freeze").

They planned to put people in a state of
suspended animation by freezing them in liquid
nitrogen…then bring them back to life when conditions
in the world and medical know-how were (presumably)
better.

In the anything-can-happen atmosphere of the 1960s,
it actually seemed plausible that scientists might be reani-
mating frozen humans in the near future. This belief was
supported by the rumor that Walt Disney had been frozen
after his death in 1966. After all, if Uncle Walt was involved, there *must* be something to it. (Note: It was just a
rumor. Disney was cremated.)

A SYMBOL OF THE MILLENNIUM

What's the connection to 2000? That was the target year enthusiasts picked for the flowering of their art. By 2000, they believed, cryonics would usher in a new golden age for humanity: "The Freezer Era."

In his 1964 book *The Prospect of Immortality*, Robert Ettinger declared: "The Freezer Era—if it develops into an age of brotherly love and a living Golden Rule, as I believe it will, may be accepted…as the embodiment of the Millennium."

A journalist reported: "Mr. Ettinger's followers propose to extend freezing throughout the world. By the year 2000 they would have several billion bodies in cold storage."

MELTDOWN

It didn't quite work out that way. In a widely publicized 1980s court case, a judge handed down a $1 million verdict against the Cryonics Society of California for allowing corpses to thaw. It's a cold world; the judgement permanently damaged their credibility.

In 1990, the authors of the book *Future Stuff* rated the chances of cryonics in the marketplace by 2000 at only 35%. Today, barring a miracle, there's no chance at all.

• **For More Information:** www.cryonics.org/

Whatever Happened to...
FLYING CARS?

*Still driving? Wouldn't you rather be doing loop-de-loops
in a skycar like the Jetsons? Back in the 1960s, a lot of
people were sure that's how we'd be getting around right
now. But we're still stuck on the ground. What happened?*

UP, UP, AND AWAY

Contrary to popular belief, flying cars do exist.
In fact, for three decades an inventor named Paul Moller
has been hard at work developing a commercial model of
his Skycar—an incredible piece of machinery. It's a
VTOL (vertical takeoff and landing) aircraft that rises
straight up from the ground, switches to "forward-thrust,"
and then climbs 7,000 feet per minute. It can to cruise at
350 mph and reach a ceiling of 30,000 feet. It even goes
900 miles between refills (gas mileage is approximately 15
mpg.)

HOW IT WORKS

According to Moller, the craft is "easier to drive than a
golf cart." He explains:

> "The three on-board computers do most of the
> work, and anybody can fly one in just two hours

or less by training on a simulator. There are only two controls: one is a lever on your left which selects altitude and rate of climb, and the other is a joystick on your right which you turn in the direction you want to go."

MOLLER AND "THE JETSONS"

If it sounds like something out of "The Jetsons," that's no coincidence. In the early 1960s, a magazine article on Moller's work caught the attention of Hanna-Barbera, the production team behind "The Jetsons." They incorporated his design into their futuristic cartoon.

Ironically, Moller's craft is now compared to the TV series it helped inspire. "If you're thinking of the Jetsons, you have the right idea," wrote The *San Diego Union-Tribune*. "The futuristic jets driven by the cartoon family are the closest thing yet to the Skycar."

COMMUTE OF THE FUTURE?

Moller thought the Skycar would be well-established by now. "It could be flying commuters to work in the millions by the year 2000," he told The *Chicago Tribune* in the late 1980s.

But he was wrong. Despite the fact that Moller had spent over $25 million developing the Skycar—and was well on his way to working out all the bugs—no major car or plane manufacturer was willing to back him financially. (Toyota and Boeing were reportedly interested at different times.)

WHAT'S GOING ON?

One critic assesses the situation:

"Moller says that all the technical problems have been solved, and that product liability and production money are the only limiting factors left. He declares: 'If sufficient funds were available, we could...be demonstrating it in a matter of months.'

"The first units produced are estimated to cost about $800,000, and he has already 80 orders, each with a $5,000 deposit. At the production rate of several thousand units per year, each would cost about $100,000. After producing around 40,000 per year, the cost would become no more than a luxury car in comparison.

"Navigating the maze of Federal Aviation Administration approvals is still ahead...but how do you think the auto industry will react to this new airborne, commuter craft? In fact, since Moller's...designs will replacé many helicopters and fixed-wing aircraft, his obstacles with powerful blocks of greedy men are only beginning."

For More Info: www.moller.com/vhistory.htm

News from 1900
AIN'T MISBEHAVIN'

This is one of the strangest articles about the millennium we've found. "Uncle Richard" apparently had a regular children's column in The Chicago Tribune. *This piece ran on December 30, 1900. Its title: "Uncle Richard Tells of the Bad Boys of the Year 2000."*

Your Uncle Richard has told you of the bad boys of many lands, and from history's dawn down to the present. He will now peer ahead into the gray mists that veil the future and tell you what is on the cards for the year 2000, and whether or not it will repay you to sit around and wish that you could be a boy at that time.

In the first place, it would not be a good idea to wish to be a bad boy in that year, for there will be no bad boys then. Inventions will have been made so wonderful that the bad boy will have to become a nice sweet child...or step off the earth.

Teachers in the schools will have wonderful instruments on the desks that will record the name of everybody who whispers, and all the teacher will have to do to bring swift punishment will be to press a certain button on the desk, and a current of electricity will shoot through the victim, and make him think he is a human pin-cushion.

Fond parents who wish their offspring to rise in the morning will not have to shout up the back stairs fifteen or twenty times and finally threaten to come "right up there now with this apple tree switch, do you hear me?" No, indeed. The parent of the year 2000 will press a small button in the sitting room, and the bed in which the boy is sleeping will have convulsions, and the boy will be hurled clear across the room. An electric spanker will then do a few stunts, and the boy will be glad to make haste in stirring himself suitably for appearance in polite society. If the boy sulks when he is downstairs his mother will punish him by not permitting him to sail with Jimmy Jones in his new airship in the afternoon.

No bad boy will run away from home to kill Indians, for there will be no Indians at that time except the ones who play football...besides nobody is going to run away if they know their fond mama is going to pursue them with the velocity and ease of the Great Bald eagle. For individual flying machines will be in great vogue that year, and mamas, as well as papas, will flit about through the air with great ease, and when they spy their offspring they will pounce down on him from some dizzying height, and bat him over the head with an aluminum wing if he says he won't promise never to smoke again.

There will be very few horses in the year 2000 and all of them will be in the dime museums, so that the small boy will have nothing to curry except the family flying machine. All the milk will be manufactured down-town and there will be no cows to drive. The milk will be forced through hydrants to the consumers and nobody will have to go after it. The fond mother will say: "James, turn on the milk at the milk-drant and let it flow for a while so that it will be cool." Will that not be an easy thing?

There will be no chores to do in the year 2000. An electric ax will split the wood and an electric shovel will put the coal into the buckets which an electric carrier will convey to the furnace. Does not all this seem too good to be true?

Of course there will be school in the

year 2000, but learning will be much easier. If the class is geography, instead of studying in the books about the capitals children will simply step into the teacher's airship and be taken on a two-hour trip through most of the capitals—Berlin, Paris, London, and Madrid—returning hurriedly and going again the next day. All the adding and multiplying and silly things like that will be done by machines and history will be learned from watching moving pictures of the events to be considered in the day's lesson. Of course, now and then some wicked boy may tie an aluminum can to a dog's tail, but the dog will probably be an electric dog, so that he will not mind the look of it at all.

Does not all of this seem like a dream? Well, dear children, you have guessed correctly, and as Uncle Richard's pipe has gone out, he will now wake up. So, good-bye.

RANDOM THOUGHT

"By the year 2000, one out of three people will be Elvis impersonators."

—Michael Sweet,
The New York Times, 1991

Uncle John's
HANDY GUIDE TO THE END OF THE WORLD
Part I

You'll hear lots of talk about the apocalypse in the next few years. Most cultures have a tradition that predicts the end of the world...and many of their prophecies could apply to our era. The good news is that they're not all fire and brimstone. Here are three examples from the East.

B UDDHISM
Background: Founded in the sixth century B.C. in India. One of its primary teachings is observance of the 10 moral precepts (standards of conduct).

Signs the End Is Near: According to the Buddha in the *Sutta-pitaka* (Buddhist scriptures and sermons):

• The 10 moral courses of conduct will disappear...and people will follow the 10 *immoral* courses instead—"theft, violence, murder, lying, evil-speaking, adultery, abusive and idle talk, covetousness and ill will, wanton greed, and perverted lust." Poverty "will grow great."

• "The Dharma [universal law, or truth] will have disappeared from the world...as a counterfeit Dharma arises."

When the World Ends: Good news! A new Buddha "by the name Maitreya" will arise. This new Buddha will "replace the counterfeit Dharma of materialism and selfishness...and give new teachings to solve the social problems of the world."

ZOROASTRIANISM

Background: A Persian religion based on the belief that the universe is filled with good and evil spirits. There will be an ultimate battle between these forces, and evil will be eliminated.

Signs the End Is Near: The *Zand-i Vohuman Yasht* predicts:

• "(At the) end of thy tenth hundredth winter...the sun is more unseen and more spotted; the year, month, and day are shorter; and the earth is more barren; and the crop will not yield the seed; and men...become more deceitful and more given to vile practices; they have no gratitude."

• "Honorable wealth will all proceed to those of perverted faith...and a dark cloud makes the whole sky night... and [it will rain] more noxious creatures than water."

When the World Ends: Saoshyant, the Man of Peace, comes to battle the forces of evil. "The resurrection of the dead will take place—the dead will rise...the world will be purged by molten metal, in which the righteous will wade as if through warm milk, and the evil will be scalded."

At the end of the battle, the Final Judgment of all souls begins. Sinners will be punished (apparently for 3 days), then forgiven, and humanity will be made immortal and free from hunger, thirst, poverty, old age, disease, and death. The world "will be made perfect once again."

HINDUISM

Background: "Hindu" is a Western term for the religious beliefs of numerous sects in India dating back to 1500 B.C. Their goal: "liberation from the cycle of rebirth and suffering."

Signs the End Is Near: The world falls into chaos and degradation; there's an increase in perversity, greed, conflict. According to Cornelia Dimmit's translation of the *Sanskrit PurAnas*:

"When deceit, falsehood, lethargy, sleepiness, violence, despondency, grief, delusion, fear, and poverty prevail... when men, filled with conceit, consider themselves equal with Brahmins...that is the *Kali Yuga* [present era]."

When the World Ends: A savior (avatar) will appear. "The Lord will again manifest Himself as the Kalki Avatar...He will establish righteousness upon the earth and the minds of the people will become pure as crystal... As a result the *Sat* or *Krta Yuga* [golden age] will be established."

$ Cashing in on 2000 $
THE MILLENNIUM FILM FESTIVAL

Ready for cheesy plots...bad acting...silly special effects? We've got the films for you!

DEATH RACE 2000 (1975). *"In the year 2000, hit-and-run driving is no longer a felony, it's a national sport!"*

Plot: Top driver "Frankenstein" (David Carradine) battles Machine Gun Joe Viterbo (Sly Stallone) to win the annual transcontinental race. The more people you run over, the better your score.

Review: A cult favorite. "Outrageous tongue-in-cheek action film...Fast-paced fun, marred by unnecessary gore." —*Leonard Maltin's Movie & Video Guide*

CHERRY 2000 (1987)
Plot: When a man accidentally short-circuits his female sex-toy robot with soap, he goes looking for replacement parts in a dangerous area called The Zone. On the way, he meets a real female—Melanie Griffith (before breast implants)—who becomes his guide.

Review: "Offbeat, occasionally funny" —*Golden Movie Retriever*

TEST-TUBE TEENS FROM THE YEAR 2000 (1993). Original title: *The Virgin Hunters*.

Plot: When sex is banned in the year 2000, horny teenagers are left with no choice but to travel though time and stop Camella Swales (Morgan Fairchild) from banning normal reproduction.

Review: "This, folks, is what low-budget video is all about." —*Video Hound's Guide to Cult Flicks and Trash Pics*

ESCAPE 2000 (1982). Original title: *Turkey Shoot*.

Plot: In the year 1995, individuality is not permitted. People who refuse to conform are labeled "deviates" and are sent to behavioral modification centers—then they're hunted in jungles for sport.

Review: "Repulsive. If constant whippings, decapitations and burnings are your idea of a good time, this one's for you." —*Movies on TV and Video Cassette*

SPACE WARRIORS 2000 (1980)

Plot / Review: "Children's special effects sci-fi with a doll coming to life to join the Galaxy Council and fight alien invaders." —*Creature Features*

All's Wells...
THAT ENDS WELLS

*A few observations from futurist H. G. Wells, author
of classic science fiction works like* War of the Worlds
and The Time Machine. *In 1901, he wrote a book of
predictions for the 20th century called* Anticipations.

RANDOM THOUGHTS
• "Human history becomes more and more a race between education and catastrophe."

• "Adapt or perish, now as ever, is Nature's inexorable imperative."

• "We live in reference to past experience, and not to future events—no matter how inevitable."

PREDICTIONS
• "Before the year A.D. 2000, and very probably before 1950, a successful aeroplane will have soared and come home safe and sound. [As soon as] that is accomplished, the new invention will be most assuredly applied to war."

• "With a neat little range, heated by electricity and provided with thermometers, with absolutely controllable temperature and proper heat screens, cooking might very easily be made a pleasant amusement [by 2000]."

Here's one of Uncle John's favorite quotes. It speaks eloquently to our time, as well.

• "People of [1901] take the railways for granted as they take the sea and sky; they were born in a railway world and they expect to die in one. But if they will strip from their eyes the most blinding of all influences—aquiescence in the familiar—they will see clearly enough that this vast and elaborate railway system of ours [is not]... likely to remain the predominant method of land-loco-motion, even for so short a period as a hundred years."

For More on Wells: www.clarndon.demon.co.uk/wells.htm *or* www.dreamwvr.com/hg_wells.htm

*   *   *

MOVIE NEWS

The earliest-documented movie with 2000 in its title is a 1909 production called *Burglary in the Year 2000*. The plot involves a professor who's invented a substance that enables objects to walk away. Two crooks steal the substance and use it to commit a series of crimes. But they drink too much wine, fall asleep, and are nabbed by the police.

Forecasting the Future
FACTS IN FICTION

Imagine that you're an average American in 1894. There are no airplanes, radios, TVs, or movies. You don't even have electricity in your house. Now imagine you encounter outlandish ideas like these in popular fiction about the year 2000. Would you scoff...or believe they were possible?

Book: *Looking Backward, 1887...2000*, by Edward Bellamy. Published in 1888.

Outlandish Idea: "There are a number of music rooms in the city, perfectly adapted acoustically to the different sorts of music. These halls are connected by telephone with all the houses of the city whose people care to pay the small fee...you can hear by merely pressing the button which will connect your house wire with the hall where it is being rendered."

And Now: We have radios.

Book: *Golf in the Year 2000*, by J.A.C.K. Published in 1892.

Outlandish Idea: "The glass on which we were to see the

golf match was dark at first; then a bell sounded and it suddenly got bright....Represented on the glass were a number of men standing about, all life-size....The effect was very curious. You saw them walking, yet they never moved from the...glass. The ground glided behind them, but...you did not notice that. They looked quite natural."

And Now: Get out the beer! It's sports on TV.

Book: *A Journey in Other Worlds*, by John Astor. Published in 1894.

Outlandish Idea: "The policemen on duty have instantaneous Kodaks mounted on tripods, which show the position of any carriage at half-and quarter-second intervals, by which it is easy to ascertain the exact speed, should the officers be unable to judge it by the eye; so there is no danger of a vehicle's speed exceeding that allowed in the section in which it happens to be; neither can a slow [vehicle] remain on the fast lines."

And now: We have radar traffic guns.

Book: *1999, An Historical Romance,* by G. D. Mitchell and H. C. Young. Published in 1898.

Outlandish Idea: "John realized that he must act quickly. He hastily placed the document before the detecting camera, which was used at the bank to photograph the faces of suspicious looking persons and questionable paper of any kind....Touching a spring, there was an electric flash that lighted up the letter—and a facsimile of it was instantaneously produced."

And Now: We have photocopy machines.

Book: *The Millennium: A Comedy of the Year 2000,* by Upton Sinclair. Published in 1903.

Outlandish Idea: "Then all at once every light in the apartment was extinguished; the next moment the room became filled with a vivid, blinding light. The guests, with their hands clasped to their heads, shrieked in agony, and collapsed upon the floor. The light faded away, and there followed utter darkness, and a hush as of a tomb...

"You drive down Broadway—it's like a string of graveyards. There are cars, cabs, motors—not a soul in them. Little piles of dust on the sidewalk—piles in the shops—piles in the cars! But not a sound! Not a fly alive!"

And Now: We have the neutron bomb (which destroys people, but not property).

Uncle John's

HANDY GUIDE TO THE PROPHETS OF DOOM #2

*If you thought the first part (page 2057)
was a downer, wait till you read this.*

G EORGE WASHINGTON
Background: That's right—the Commander-in-Chief of the Colonial Army during the Revolutionary War—America's first president (1789–1796)—is also a celebrated Prophet of Doom.

One day during the Revolutionary War, when he was alone in his office, a beautiful woman appeared out of nowhere. George thought she was the Grim Reaper, but she said: "Son of the Republic, look and learn." As he watched, the room disappeared; he saw a vision of the world of 1999 spread out in front of him.

Doomsday 2000: Then the *really* weird stuff started happening. A dark angel cast a black cloud over America; there were flashes of lightning; people started screaming in agony. Then a dark cloud came from Africa and covered America again "with its ill omen." Black clouds covered other countries too, each with a red light at the center. And through the lights, Washington could see massive armies gathering. Then they sailed across the ocean and overwhelmed America. There was a huge battle; then the angel sprinkled water over the world, and there was peace.

Believability Factor: Who are we to argue with the Father of Our Country? On the other hand, he *did* grow hemp.

THE GREAT PYRAMID

Background: No one is sure who built the Great Pyramid in Egypt, or why they did it. Most historians speculate that it was a tomb for Khufu (Cheops), monarch of the Fourth Dynasty, about 4,000 to 5,000 years ago. Other opinions range from a landing pad for UFOs to a showcase for the skills of Atlanteans (who were "technological advisors" to the Egyptians).

In 1971, Peter Tompkins published his best-selling book *Secrets of the Great Pyramid*. In it, he contended that the pyramid was more than a tomb—it was an instrument that could accurately predict the future.

"It seemed to me that nobody would build such an enormity just for a tomb," he said. "It had to have some other function."

After years of research, Tompkins found what he was looking for in the forgotten theories of Piazzi Smyth.

The Pyramid Inch. In 1864, Smyth, a royal astronomer of Scotland who'd entered the King's Chamber of the Great Pyramid, made his "shocking" discovery:

If you measure the passages inside the pyramid, starting from its lowest point (an outside corner) and moving to its center (the King's Chambers), you'll find a timeline of important events in Western history.

Each time the passage turns or branches off, it symbolizes an historic milestone.

However, in order to make this work, you have to use a special unit of measurement that is one one-thousandth of an inch longer than a standard inch (1.001"). Smyth called it the "pyramid inch," but some people say it's historically known as the "sacred Jewish inch."

Doomsday 2000: Smyth decided that the starting point on the timeline was around 4,000 B.C.; tracing it to the King's chamber, he found that it ended ominously at 2001 A.D. This suggests to pyramidologists that something cataclysmic is going to happen soon.

Believability Factor: Which pyramidologist do you want to believe? Some, for example, used the pyramid to forecast the Second Coming of Christ in 1881. Then they changed the date to 1936...and then to 1953. Nowadays the pyramid folks seem to place the end of the world at anywhere from 1999 to 2001, depending on whose interpretation you read. One author even claims that the date September 17, 2001 is written on a stone slab in the center chamber.

However, it's hard to explain the Great Pyramid. Some details about the structure cited by "experts" are mindboggling. If they're accurate...well, anything could be true about it. For example:

• The pyramid is located at "the exact center of the Earth's landmass....The odds of its having been built where it is are 1 in 3 billion."

• "The height of the pyramid's apex is 5,812.98", and each side is 9,131" from corner to corner (in a straight line). If the circumference of the pyramid is divided by twice its height (the diameter of a circle is twice the radius), the result is 3.14159, which just happens to be pi."

• "The average height of land above sea level...as can be measured only by modern-day satellites and computers, happens to be 5,449 inches. That is the exact height of the pyramid."

There's a lot more, and frankly, it's all pretty amazing For a structure built 4,000 years ago. So maybe the publisher of a newsletter called *Pyramid Power 2000* is onto something when she says: "In 2000, the whole world will be watching the pyramids for a clue to our future." Anyway, it's better than watching TV.

For More On Pyramids: www.primenet.com/~kjohnson/

Introducing...
THE AMAZING MECHANICAL VALET

In 1903, an American journalist wrote this article and puckishly attributed it to The Scientific American magazine. He dated it May 28, 1999.

THE MECHANICAL FIGURE THAT DOES EVERYTHING BUT FEED ITS OWNER

Some years ago the need of a machine which would dress persons on arising from bed, make their toilet and prepare them for breakfast, or a stroll on the street, was generally felt.

Several attempts were made to supply this want, but nothing was perfected until M. Pantalon announced the completion of his automatic valet. This machine was shaped very much like an ordinary man, except that it was built on an absolutely square plan. There were two upholstered legs, a heavy, square chest, and a square head, resembling a block.

MECHANISM OF THE VALET

The machinery was directly in the center of the chest, controlling the movement of the legs and arms. Instead of a face, the head bore a clock-dial. The whole valet was wound up by a small crank in the back. If a man wished to be aroused at 8 o'clock in the morning, he adjusted the alarm button on a small dial on the face of the clock. Promptly at 8 o'clock the alarm in the head of the valet exploded, waking the sleeper.

The first movement on the part of the valet after the alarm had sounded was to move quickly but noiselessly in the direction of the bathroom, where, by automatic stoppers, the water is set running, stopping instantly on the tub being filled.

AUTOMATIC BATH

After turning on the water, the valet moved back to the bed, threw the covers aside, and with one of its automatic arms gently lifted the man from his resting place, conveyed him to the bath room, and immersed him.

The bath completed, the valet drew from its chest-cupboard two towels, with which it briskly rubbed the bather, and then again lifting him up carried him back into the bedroom, where it proceeded to dress him in clothes which had been laid in a certain place the night before.

From its automatic chest the valet took comb, brush and whisk broom, and in less time than would be ordinarily consumed in telling about it, the toilet was completed. A feature of the invention, as perfected by Pantalon, was the arrangement on the time dial by which the speed of the valet could be regulated, and a man could be dressed quickly or slowly, as he preferred. For busy men, M. Pantalon has invented valets that do the business in less than three minutes, including bath. The chief value of these valets is that, not being human, they cannot gossip, and every man may become a hero to his valet, provided the valet is automatic.

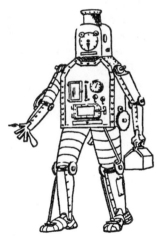

Millennium Clocks
COUNTDOWN TO 2000

*We use atomic clocks to find out precisely when
2000 begins (see page 2071). But we use countdown
clocks to build drama as the Big Day gets closer.
Of course, it helps if they work.*

VIVE LE MILLENNIUM!

The first countdown clock to arrive was also the
first to go. After its official kickoff by French President
François Mitterand (see page 2132), the clock at the
Pompidou Center—which resembles a soccer goalpost—
was booted into oblivion. Apparently, its builders could
count down to the future, but not plan for it. When
renovations began on the Center in the 1990s, the clock
had to be dismantled and put into storage. Talk about
white elephants—the French government has tried to
give it away, but so far, no takers. (Germany, for one, has
already turned it down.)

CHIME IN THE SLIME

In 1994, the National Lottery of Ireland announced a
"Countdown 2000" contest to design a "Millennium
Timer" that would tick backward until 2000. The design
that won in 1996 was called "the most beautiful and

astonishing clock in the world" at its unveiling. It is a nine-digit timer that floated just beneath the surface of the river Liffey, which cuts through Dublin.

However, the clock has been pulled from the river, because the murky water prevented people from reading the digits—earning it the nickname "chime in the slime." An *Irish Times* writer said it was "like inviting your guests to admire the family silver when it was floating in a greasy sink."

THE MILLENNIUM WALL-CLOCK

In March 1980, the Chinese government built a millennium countdown clock on the Great Wall, just northwest of Beijing. The clock—whose face is 26 square meters—is supposed to inspire the nation to "seize the moment to build up the motherland."

AN EVEN BIGGER BEN

A futuristic clock to mark the year 2000 in England is being planned by Robert Eden, grandson of former prime minister Anthony Eden. The "people's clock" will be 60 feet high and feature a digital panel of six numbers counting down each second until 2000. A "rocket" on four stilts will descend to the ground at the big moment, as video panels broadcast other historic events. The clock will be placed outside the Science Museum in London.

Important Influence #3:
NOSTRADAMUS

*Could Nostradamus have predicted his own influence four
centuries after he died? Probably not. This 16th-century
soothsayer is still as popular as ever—thanks, in part,
to his cryptic predictions about the 20th century.*

CLAIM TO FAME He's the father of apocalyptic
prophecy for the millennium. The Bible gave us
frightening imagery in *Revelation*, but Nostradamus gave
us a specific date to fear: the 7th month of 1999.

BACKGROUND Michel de Nostradame was born in
1503 in St. Remy, France. He was trained as a physician
and gained a reputation for "remarkable healing powers"
during the Black Plague. But when his wife and two in-
fant sons died of the plague, he gave up medicine and began wandering aimlessly through the south of France.

About this time, Nostradamus began experiencing visions and discovered his "powers of prophecy." According
to legend, he spontaneously knelt before a monk named
Felice Peretti—later Pope Sixtus V—and insisted that
one day he would head the Catholic Church.

After years of studying magic and astrology, Nostradamus began publishing an almanac filled with predictions

in 1550. Thanks to his almanacs, his reputation as a psychic spread. And in 1558, he published the book that sealed his reputation: *Centuries.*

Centuries was Nostradamus's masterwork—a series of 1,000 quatrains (four-line verses) that purported to predict events until the year 3797.

IMPACT THEN According to *The Book of Predictions:* "In his own day Nostradamus was acknowledged as the greatest seer alive."

"His neighbors held him in awe and respect," writes Stewart Robb in *Prophecies on World Events by Nostradamus.* "Kings, princes and prelates beat a path to his door; he was never in want...he died a prophet with honor in his own country."

One quatrain in particular catapulted Nostradamus to psychic superstardom in his own time:

> The young lion will overcome the old one
> On the field of battle in combat:
> He will put out his eyes in a cage of gold,
> Two wounds one, then die a cruel death.

As it turns out, a few years later, the reigning French monarch, Henry II (the "old lion"), was mortally wounded in a riding tournament by a young captain of the Scottish guard (the "young lion").

The details of the event were so similar to the quatrain that the king's wife, Queen Catherine de Medici, was sure Nostradamus had prophesied it. She invited him into her royal circle, and he began devising royal horoscopes and offering advice based on astrological events.

By the time he died in 1566, Nostradamus was a legend. Tales of his death only added to his stature. On the night he died, he reportedly told a pupil that "tomorrow at sunrise I shall not be here." He also supposedly arranged for a marble plaque to be buried with him. When his coffin was exhumed in 1700 to move his remains to a newer tomb, the plaque was discovered on his skeleton. On it, the story goes, the date "1700" was inscribed.

IMPACT NOW Even if you think Nostradamus's prophecies are nonsense, you can't dismiss him as a cultural force. The word *prediction*, for example, was reportedly first coined in a 1561 critique of Nostradamus's work. And *Centuries* has never been out of print. After the Bible, it's the oldest continuously published book in history—still widely read, interpreted…and believed.

A few examples of Nostradamus's contemporary influence:

• A 1980 book by Jean Charles de Fontbrune, *Nostradamus: Historien et Prophete*, created a sensation in France with the claim that Nostradamus predicted an

Arab attack on Europe that would soon trigger World War III. A poll conducted by *Paris Match* revealed that 75% of French citizens had heard of the book and 25% (17 million people) believed it.

• In 1988, a "mini-crisis" occurred in California when *The Man Who Saw Tomorrow*—a documentary about Nostradamus hosted by Orson Welles—predicted that a terrible earthquake would imminently destroy Los Angeles. Gossip columnists reported that so many celebrities had left town, it was easy to get good tables at Hollywood restaurants.

• In 1991, Japanese author Ben Goto reached the top of his country's bestseller list with *Predictions of Nostradamus: Middle East Chapter*, which purported to show how Nostradamus had predicted events leading to the Gulf War.

In recent years, Nostradamus has become a tabloid star. A typical headline in the *Weekly World News*: "New! Secret Predictions of Nostradamus! The Date Jesus Will Return To Earth...& Bring Peace To The Planet!"

What is Nostradamus's connection to the millennium? One of the only quatrains in *Centuries* that mentioned a specific date referring to the "terror" that was to come from the sky in the seventh month of 1999. Hundreds of books have been written which begged people to listen to Nostradamus's "warning."

"We are the people to whom Nostradamus wanted to speak," write Hewitt and Lorie in *Nostradamus—The End of the Millennium*. "[We're] the generation to whom he speaks clearly for the first time."

A bewildered publishing executive once told Uncle John: "It's amazing, but it seems that we just can't lose money doing books about Nostradamus."

And other Nostradamus products are hitting the market in time for the millennium. Notable items include a Nostradamus 900 number, and a Nostradamus watch to countdown to 2000. This is particularly ironic, because if Nostradamus was right, we may not make it! (For details, see "Prophets of Doom" on page 2200.)

For More On Nostradamus: www.dreamscape.com/ morgana/titan.htm *or* www.dalnet.se/~star/nostre.htm

*　　　*　　　*

"In 2,000 years, the greatest thing mankind ever devised, I think, in my humble opinion, is Saran Wrap."
—**Mel Brooks, 2000-Year-Old Man**

"I'll be astounded if this planet is still going fifty years from now. I don't think we will reach 2000. It would be miraculous!"
—**Alistair Cooke**

Trivia 2000
MILLENNIANA

*Want some more useless bits of info about
2000? You've come to the right page...*

C OINCIDENCE?
The "Decade of the Brain" (Proclamation 6158 by
the U.S. Congress) went into effect on July 17, 1990. It
ends on December 31, 1999.

RUSSIAN ROULETTE
According to an opinion poll published in 1990 in the
Moscow News, Jesus Christ will exert the greatest influence over Russian citizens in the year 2000. Christ
polled 58%; Lenin was in 2nd place, with 36%.

COLLECTOR'S ITEM
The first (and perhaps only) year 2000 concept record:
"Into Outer Space with Lucia Pamela in the Year 2000."
It was recorded "on the moon" by Pamela and a few musical friends. ("The air is so thin that everything sounds
different up there," she reports.) What does it sound
like? Critics describe it as "the sound of a ragtime band
lost in another galaxy, hopelessly whacked out on alien
hallucinogens."

The Millennium Book Club
SCIENCE FICTION 2000

*No book about the millennium would be complete
without mentioning some of the science-fiction classics
that have already brought the year 2000 to life for
millions of readers. Here are five of our favorites.*

THE MARTIAN CHRONICLES, by Ray Bradbury (1950)

Plot: After several failed attempts, Earthlings finally
reach Mars in 1999. They bring with them loneliness,
alienation, prejudice, greed and pollution—the same
problems that beset them on Earth. By 2001, all the
Martians are dead—wiped out by chicken
pox. The humans who remain slowly destroy the environment. When anthropologist Jeff Spender is sent to investigate, he
asks another character: "Isn't it enough
they've ruined one planet, without ruining another?"

THE DOOR INTO SUMMER, by Robert A. Heinlein (1957)

Plot: In 1970, Dan Davis, an electronic engineer, is perfecting his new invention—a
household robot named Flexible Frank. But

behind his back, Davis is being swindled by his business partners and fiancée.

Depressed, Davis decides to take a "long sleep"—i.e., be cryonically frozen. He awakens in the "fast new world" of 2000 with many questions: "Have they reached the stars yet? Who's cooking up 'The War to End War' this time? Do babies come out of test tubes?" To his surprise and delight, he discovers time travel has been perfected. This means he can seek revenge in 1970 and rescue his beloved cat Pete.

ECOTOPIA, by Ernest Callenbach (1975)

Plot: In 1999, reporter Will Weston is dispatched to Ecotopia, an independent country whose territory includes the states of Washington and Oregon as well as Northern California.

The environment is the number one concern in Ecotopia—every conceivable legal measure has been passed to protect it. Weston discovers a fiercely independent, politically correct community that slowly draws him in.

MAKE ROOM! MAKE ROOM! by Harry Harrison (1966)

Plot: Overpopulation and intense heat combine in the summer of 1999 to put New York City on the edge of catastrophe. People have become increasingly desperate;

water and food shortages, social unrest, and predictions of doomsday fill the air. Meanwhile, Detective Andy Rusch is ordered to find Billy Chung, a teenager who accidentally committed murder when he broke into the luxury apartment of a syndicate boss. A cat-and-mouse chase ensues through the disaster-plagued streets of the city. (Note: This novel inspired the film *Soylent Green*.)

LOOKING BACKWARD, FROM THE YEAR 2000, by Mack Reynolds (1973)

Plot: An updated version of Edward Bellamy's *Looking Backward* (see page 2121). This time, Julian West has a heart condition and is "frozen" for 30 years, until science can cure him. When he awakes in 2000, he finds a technologically advanced, egalitarian society in which everyone is wealthy. The earth is "park-like and beautiful. Most people pass the time as eternal students, plugged into the national computer banks which keep them abreast of all human knowledge." Admirable affirmation of a classic utopian vision.

* * *

"The only new idea that could save humanity in the 21st century is for women to take over the management of the world."
—Gabriel Garcia Marquez

Look How Far We've Come
A VIEW FROM 1901

*We've come a long way in just 200 years—from the horse
and buggy to space shuttles...from goose quill pens to laser
printers...from gunpowder to atomic bombs. This
article was written in 1901. How would
you bring it up to date?*

B ACKGROUND In the January 1901 edition of *Popular Science*, a well-known professor wrote, "If any century ever had cause to boast of its accomplishments, surely the one now ended has more cause than all of them together." To prove it, he compared the state of progress in 1800 with that of 1900. His article is fascinating, especially because it points out how much the world of 2000 owes to the inventive spirit of the 19th century. Here are some of the professor's examples:

☞ "We [the 19th century] received [from the 18th century] the horse and ox; we bequeath [to the 20th century] the locomotive, the automobile, and the bicycle."

☞ "We received the goose quill; we bequeath the fountain pen and the typewriter."

☞ "We received the sail ship, six weeks to Europe; we bequeath the steamship, six days to Europe."

☛ "We received the staircase; we bequeath the elevator."

☛ "We received gunpowder; we bequeath nitroglycerin."

☛ "We received the hand loom; we bequeath the cotton gin and woolen mill."

☛ "We received the leather fire bucket; we bequeath the steam fire engine."

☛ "We received wood and stone structures; we bequeath 20-storied steel structures."

☛ "We received the painter's brush and easel; we bequeath lithography and photography."

☛ "We received the past as silent; we bequeath the phonograph, and the voices of the dead may again be heard."

☛ "We received pain as an allotment to man; we bequeath ether, chloroform, and cocaine."

☛ "We received two dozen members of the solar system; we bequeath 500."

☛ "We received Johnson's Dictionary with 20,000 words; we bequeath he modern dictionary with 240,000 words."

☛ "We received unlimited dependence on muscles; we bequeath automatic mechanisms."

☞ "We received the tallow dip; we bequeath the incandescent light."

☞ "We received a million stars; we bequeath 100 million."

☞ "We received weather unannounced. We bequeath the weather bureau."

☞ "We received gangrene; we bequeath antiseptic surgery."

☞ "We received decomposition helplessly; we bequeath cold storage."

☞ "We received foods for immediate consumption; we bequeath the canning industry."

☞ "We received the products of distant countries as rarities; we bequeath them as bountiful as home productions."

☞ "We received history as events remembered and recorded; we bequeath the kinetoscope [cinema]."

Who'll Still Be Here?

...MISSED IT BY THAT MUCH!

Ever wonder whether you'd survive to the year 2000?
Congratulations—it looks like you have. But not
everyone did. Here are a few famous folks who
have dropped out of the race already.

HENRY MANCINI

Claim to Fame: Two-time Oscar winner, composer of "Moon River" and "The Pink Panther Theme"

Secret Dream: At a testimonial dinner on his 70th birthday in 1994, he rose and told the audience "More than anything, I'd like to be with you at the millennium." He finished his remarks with: "Let's get to the year 2000 and worry from there, okay?"

Outcome: Two months later, he was dead.

GRACE HOPPER

Claim to Fame: Pioneer in the field of data processing. She co-developed the computer language COBOL and coined the word "bug" for mysterious computer problems.

The first is that the party on December 31, 1999 will be a New Year's Eve party to end all New Year's Eve parties.

The second is that I want to point back to the early days of computers and say to all the doubters, 'See? We told you the computers could do that.'"

Outcome: She died in 1992.

ISAAC ASIMOV

Claim to Fame: One of the most prolific modern science writers and a giant of science fiction

Secret Dream: In the introduction to *I, Asimov,* he wrote: "It was my notion that I ought to wait until the symbolic year of 2000 (always so important to science fiction writers and futurists) and write my autobiography then. However, I will be 80 years old in 2000, and it may just be possible that I may not make it."

Outcome: He died in 1992. Fortunately for his fans, he'd decided not to wait and had already completed the book. It was published in 1994.

For More On Asimov: www.clark.net/pub/edseiler/WWW/asimov_home_page.html

• • •

"We appreciate that the turning of the year 2000 represents some sort of continuum from the perspective of our white brothers, but to us it is just another day."

—*Prof. Oren Lyons, Onandaga Nation*

Predictions from the Past
"COMMUTING WILL BE A PLEASURE IN 2000!"

Ever been stuck in traffic on your way home? People from the mid-1900s would've been shocked by our traffic jams—they were sure that by now we'd have simple, stress-free commuting in...

R EMOTE-CONTROL CARS
"However the [businessman of 2000] travels...he will not be obliged to handle the controls by himself. He may well be able to doze or read, while, from a distant point, his car or plane will be held on its course by short-wave impulses."

—Arthur Train, Jr.,
The Story of Everyday Things (1941)

"AERIAL BUSES"
"[In 2000], commuters will go to the city, a hundred miles away, in huge aerial busses that hold 200 passengers. Hundreds of thousands more will make such journeys twice a day in their own helicopters."

—Waldemar Kaempfert,
Popular Mechanics, 1950

ENCLOSED CAPSULES

"[Commuters will] rent small four-seater capsules such as we find on a ski lift. These capsules will be linked together into little trains that come into the city. As the train goes out towards the perimeter of the city, the capsule will become an individual unit. One can then drive to wherever he may want to go."

—Ulrich Frantzen,
Prophecy for the Year 2000
(1967)

"AIR-CUSHION COACHES"

A West Coast executive could commute 300 miles to Los Angeles with ease. "He might board his reserved-seat air-cushion coach at 8:15 a.m. It would lift off the roadbed, whirl around an 'acceleration loop' and plunge into the main tube running from Seattle to San Diego. Little more than half an hour later, the car would peel off onto the 'deceleration loop' in downtown Los Angeles. By 9 a.m. the executive would be at his desk."

—Mitchell Gordon,
*Here Comes Tomorrow! Living and
Working in the Year 2000* **(1966)**

Mark Your Calendar
STAY TUNED...

*What happens after December 31, 1999? Well, if
the apocalypse or Y2K don't get us, there will be lots
of special events to look forward to. For example:*

JUBILEE 2000—Rome, Italy

What It Is: A year-long celebration sponsored by the Roman Catholic Church, billed as "'A Year of Grace for the Church and for the World'...to recall and to celebrate the memory of the Incarnation of the Son of God." Pope John Paul II has described the celebration as a "new Advent" and the "greatest Church event of the 20th century."

Vital Stats: Starts on Christmas Eve 1999; focus is on the symbolic birth of Jesus Christ. Major events include an International Eucharistic Congress and a World Youth Rally. The Pope may also visit Jerusalem.

For More Info: www.xibalba.com/solt/jubilee/index.html

EARTH DAY 2000—Global

What It Is: The 30th anniversary of Earth Day. Local events emphasize on sustainability and renewing environmental awareness in the new millennium.

Vital Stats: Takes place on April 22. More than 300 mil-

lion people in 150 nations are expected to join in.
For More Info: www.cfe.cornell.edu/Earthday/

SUMMER OLYMPICS 2000—Sydney, Australia

What It Is: The 27th modern Olympics. According to a
spokesperson, "We have tied our environmental policies
into the millennium as a package to take us to the future."
Examples: An Olympic Park is being constructed on re-
claimed industrial land; a "solar" Athletes Village is being
designed according to "strict environmental guidelines."
Vital Stats: Runs September 15 (opening ceremony) to
October 1. Athletes from 200 countries are expected to
take part. Estimated worldwide audience: 3.5 billion.
For More Info: www.sydney.olympic.org/

EXPO 2000—Hannover, Germany

What It Is: A huge World's Fair covering 1.7 million
square meters. Theme: *Humankind-Nature-Technology.*
"We are especially interested in millennium observances
that will be using the renewal properties of the year 2000
to move the world toward a more sustainable, peaceful,
just, and humane future," says a spokesperson.

Vital Stats: Runs June 1 to October 31. At least 143
countries have agreed to participate; 40 million people
are expected to visit the fair.

For More Info: www.expo2000.de/index-e.html

And Now Back To...
"AS THE AIRSHIP FLIES"

A Soap Opera from 1903

The setting: An airship in the year 2000. The characters: Everson Lumley, a dashing time-traveler from 1900, and Miss Tibjul, a woman assigned to show him the city. It's nighttime. As we look in on the couple, Miss Tibjul breathlessly says...

"This is the hour, dear Lumley, when lovers take ship and sail through space."

The voice faded in a deep sigh.

Lumley coughed in an embarrassed way. Why did she "dear" him...and what sort of emotion lay behind that sigh? He wished the [robot] piloting the airship would hurry and get them to their destination.

"Courtship," she continued, "is all very different in our day, Lumley, from what it was in yours."

"Yes?" returned Lumley faintly.

"Indeed it is. Then men did the wooing and the proposing. A woman might lose her heart, but false pride prevented her from speaking to the object of her affections, and too often that object went off and married some other girl. Think of the broken-hearted woman, dear Lumley, who was thus made a victim of foolish convention. *Now* if a woman cares for a man, and desires his hand in marriage, she does not now hesitate to say so."

Lumley was shivering. He wanted to say something, and even tried to, but no sound came when his lips framed the words.

"Did you sigh, Lumley?" whispered Miss Tibjul.

Lumley made some incoherent reply.

"Everson," went on Miss Tibjul, "I feel as though I must tell you what is on my mind. Do you think you could ever care—"

TO BE CONTINUED?

This passage is from William Wallace Cook's 1903 novel, A Round Trip to the Year 2000.

Important Influence #4
EDWARD BELLAMY

One of the most popular authors of the 19th century,
Bellamy set his bestselling book in the year 2000.
Chances are you've never heard of it...or him.

CLAIM TO FAME Bellamy's 1888 bestseller, *Looking Backward 2000...1887*, was the first popular book to portray the millennium as a "golden age" of human achievement. As a direct result of his work, 2000 came to symbolize, in the popular imagination, a place in time where people's dreams for the future might actually be realized.

BACKGROUND Little in Bellamy's early life hinted at future celebrity. After studying law in New York in 1871, he passed the bar...then abandoned his law practice to work at a Massachusetts newspaper.

When an illness forced him to leave journalism, he turned to fiction. His first two novels flopped. His third, *Looking Backward*, was set in a utopian society in the year 2000; he used it as a plot vehicle to dramatize the economic and social reforms he thought America needed.

Looking Backward. By today's standards, *Looking Back-*

ward's plot is pretty hokey. The hero, Julian West, is hypnotized for insomnia…and stays asleep for 113 years. He awakes in Boston in the year 2000, and is befriended by Dr. Leete, who leads him on a tour of the city explaining how the problems of the late 19th century have been solved.

Bellamy described futuristic marvels such as TV, radio, and credit cards ("An American credit card is just as good in Europe as gold used to be," he wrote). But it was his blueprint for a "perfect society" that captivated readers in 1888. Under a new political system called "nationalism," ownership of companies was shared by all—there was no unemployment, no war, no violence, no money. There were no lawyers, no banks, and no jails.

IMPACT THEN *Looking Backward* was a surprise hit. Within a year of its publication, it had become the third bestselling novel of the 19th century—behind only *Uncle Tom's Cabin* and *Ben-Hur*. It was translated into more than twenty languages and eventually sold more than a million copies.

"It's a socialist tract," says a critic, "and a persuasive one. Part of its appeal was that it awakened Americans to the possibilities of change. It won converts to socialism by making it respectable, exciting, and desirable."

Bellamy became a household name; more than 150 "Bellamy Clubs" were formed around the U.S. to put his ideas into action. And he inspired a new generation of writers, planners and politicians—including a young Franklin Delano Roosevelt. Bellamy even started a new political party based on the socialist ideas in *Looking Backward*— the Nationalist Party.

Bellamy (who died in 1896) was lionized...vilified... and plagiarized. Between 1888 and 1900, approximately 150 utopian novels set in the year 2000 were written in the United States. Many were carbon copies of *Looking Backward*. All helped perpetuate his legacy...for a while. After World War I, Bellamy's ideas were considered "irrelevant."

IMPACT NOW Today, hardly anyone has ever heard of Bellamy's book. (Have you?) On the 100th anniversary of its publication, Warren Sloat wrote a devastating critique in The *New York Times*, pointing out how far off Bellamy had been with most of his predictions.

Still, he's an important figure. L. S. Klepp of the *Village Voice* calls *Looking Backward* "the most popular and influential fictional utopia ever written." And futurist Gail Collins adds: "Looking backward now from Bellamy's future, the saddest thing is not that we have failed to create the utopia he imagined, but that we have stopped dreaming up utopias of our own."

For More On Bellamy: oak.cats.ohiou.edu/~aw148888/ bellamy.html

Trivia 2000
MILLENNIANA

*More factoids for millennium trivia
buffs. Get 'em while they're hot!*

TIME FLIES Dick Clark, America's perennial teenager, will be 70 years old in 2000.

APOCALYPSE WHEN? An encouraging note to skeptics: Christopher Columbus believed the apocalypse was imminent. But he calculated that the world would end in 1656...not 2000.

MILLENNIUM FEVER By 1997, New York City's Rainbow Room had sold out all 200 advance seats for New Year's Eve, 1999 and had a waiting list of 850 people. Estimated cost for the evening: $1,000 a person, not including beverages, tips, or taxes.

HUH? According to a 1994 *Cosmopolitan* article, the "Cosmo Girl" in the year 2000 will be "an egg-freezing, libido-boosting dynamo with no glass ceiling, preparing for missions to Mars or donning the virtual-reality goggles for a shopping spree."

Looney Tunes and

THE MEANING OF
THE MILLENNIUM

*Believe it or not, one expert insists that a 1944 Bugs
Bunny cartoon called "The Old Grey Hare" portrays
"the essence of modern society's relationship with
the year 2000." Here's how he explains it.*

There are three stages of consciousness.

STAGE I
We see 2000 as a manifestation of God's will.

Elmer (who represents the masses) is unhappy with his
life. He's ready to give up...but he has a spiritual experience—he talks with God. Elmer believes God is telling
him that his problems will be solved in a distant future
called "2000 A.D."

Elmer Fudd (*crying bitterly*): "Aw-ahwahwah. I twy and I
twy. But I just can't seem to catch that o-o-old wabbit."

Voice of God: "If at first you don't succeed, Elmer, try try
again."

Elmer: "Twy twy agin? Yeah, but how long will it take?"

God: "Come, Elmer, Let us look fa-a-ar far into the future...Come, Elmer...Past the year 1950...1960...Past 1970... 80...90....(*switches to telephone operator voice*) When you hear the sound of the gong, it will be exactly 2000."

*Flashes of lighting and smoke. Elmer is suddenly an
old man with glasses and a white mustache.*

STAGE II
We move from faith in God to faith in science.

Elmer: "Hey, where am I? What happened? I'm all win-kled. Hey, what year is this? (*picks up a newspaper*)...2000 A.D.? What's this? Gwacious. Smellovision replaces tele-vison? Holy mackwel! Where's my wifle? Here it is. (*picks up a futuristic-looking weapon*) Whaa-at? (*reads*) 'Buck Wodgers Wightning Quick Wabbit Killer?' Oh boy! Now let me at the widdle wabbit! Lemme at him! I'll wiquidate him! Lemme at him! Where's that wabbit? Where's that wabbit?"

STAGE III
We realize that no matter what century it is,
we still have to deal with the same old "bugs."

*A geriatric Bugs Bunny with a cane and a
bushy white beard pops out of the ground.*

BUGS (*in a crackly voice*): "Eh-h-h, what's up, Prune-face?"

Although it's far in the future, Bugs and Elmer play out the same old interaction:

- Elmer tries to kill Bugs with his new rifle.
- Bugs pretends he's hit and cons the remorseful Elmer into digging a grave.
- Bugs then shovels dirt into it, burying Elmer alive.

"Well anyway," Elmer says, surprisingly calm, "that pesty wabbit is out of my life forever and ever!"

Bugs pops through the dirt wall, grinning. "Well, now...I wouldn't say tha-a-at!"

That's all, folks!

* * *

RANDOM THOUGHT

"Either man won't be on the earth or he will have used his brain in a very big way by the year 2000."

—**Buckminster Fuller**

Forecasting the Future
THE AMAZING
"SIR ORACLE"

Practically every luminary of the late 19th century
made predictions for the 20th. Most were laughably
off-target, but every once in a while someone showed
an extraordinary gift to "see" into the future.
One of these was David Goodman Croly.

BACKGROUND In 1888, an obscure little volume
with a long title—*Glimpses of the Future, Suggestions
As to the Drift of Things (To Be Read Now and Judged in the
Year 2000)*—appeared on bookshelves.

Ever heard of it? Its author, David Goodman Croly
(who died shortly after its publication), was a newspaper
columnist known as "Sir Oracle." Today, his work is considered a milestone in predictive literature. Historian I. F.
Clarke calls him "one of the early American pioneers in
writing about the future."

Here are some of his predictions:

TELECOMMUNICATIONS: "In the year 2000, it will
not be necessary to go to a meeting to hear a political
orator, or to a church to be edified by a fine discourse, or

to a concert hall to hear the noblest instrumental or vocal music. The telephone and the graphophone [sic] will be so perfected that we can enjoy these pleasures at our own homes."

THE GREEN MOVEMENT: "No one should be allowed to cut down a tree without planting another in its place. Our wasteful destruction of forests is almost a crime against the generations that are to follow us."

DESKTOP PUBLISHING: "It looks to me as if the journal of the future will dispense with the compositor or typesetter. The artist will be employed as well as the writer and their sketches and text will be photographs put on gelatin, or some similar menstruum, and multiplied ad infinitum. This would revolutionize the whole art of printing."

TABLOID JOURNALISM: "It is sickening to take up a newspaper and read of murders, or of railroad and marine disasters, the abandonment of wives by their husbands and vice-versa...but it must be confessed that readers crave this kind of literary pablum."

NEGATIVE CAMPAIGNING: "The average politician wants to offend no one; and this is why negative presidential candidates and 'dark horses' take the place of really able statesmen in our quadrennial contests."

NO-FAULT DIVORCE: "Marriage is no longer a religious rite even in Catholic countries, but a civil contract, and the logical result would seem to be a state of public opinion which would justify a change of partners whenever the contracting couple mutually agreed to separate."

CAREERS FOR WOMEN: "Women are largely beginning to support themselves; they are being educated with that view. Those who enter a lucrative calling do not care to be the wives of men who cannot keep up the standard of comfort they have set for themselves. Hence there are great classes of women beginning to take part in our modern life who are not dependent on the other sex."

LEGAL REFORM: "Our tedious legal forms waste the time and money of a very busy people. Our Supreme Court is three years and a half behind its business. Every murderer can now have two or three trials. Thus time is wasted and costs continue to increase. By-and-by the people will not stand it, and a social convulsion may result."

CORPORATE MERGERS: "The larger commercial movements of the age in all civilized countries are tending to mass wealth in fewer hands and to decrease the numbers and influence of the middle classes. Look at the great stores in all the capitals of the world!...These have driven out the small storekeeper, because they can give a better article for a lower price...the brain-work of the business world is destined in time to be represented by a very few great firms, who will practically be in control of the wealth of the several nations."

AIR TRANSPORTATION: "Aerial navigation will solve the mystery of the poles, and eventually there will be no "dark region" on any of the continents. Of course all this seems very wild, but we live in an age of scientific marvels, and the navigation of the air, if accomplished, would be the most momentous event of all ages....If the *aerostat* should become as cheap for travelers as the sailing vessel, why may not man become migratory, like the birds, occupying the more mountainous regions and sea-coast in summer and more tropical climes in winter."

CONCLUSION

"I believe most profoundly the final triumph of good over evil—and yet, all is chaos. But the duty of every human being is to help hasten the day when man and his environment will be brought into harmonious relations with each other."

Uncle John's Top 15
POP MILESTONES

*Over the last 40 years, a handful of diehards have
been quietly laying the groundwork for the coming
pop phenomenon of 2000. Here's our Top 15
list of pop firsts for the millennium.*

1957: FIRST HOTEL RESERVATION. Inspired by a
novel about soldiers who agree to meet at New York's
Waldorf-Astoria Hotel if they survive WWII, Jim Hoogerwert and two friends made a pact to meet at the Waldorf
on December 31, 1999. Hoogerwert, who will be 56 in
1999, told The *Los Angeles Times* in 1993: "I could never
imagine, then, being 56. It just seemed so far off."

1955 ▬▬▬ **1960** ▬▬▬

**1963: FIRST YEAR 2000
ORGANIZATION.** The World Association for Celebrating the Year 2000 (WACY) was founded in England
by John Goodman. It's now a worldwide foundation with
members in 30 countries, but Goodman's going to miss
the Big Day—he died in 1994, at age 65.

1966: FIRST YEAR 2000 TIME CAPSULE.
The Mutual of New York Insurance Company buried a time capsule outside the doorway of its Syracuse, New York office building, to be opened in the year 2000.

1969: FIRST #1 SONG. The Fifth Dimension's version of "The Age of Aquarius," was #1 for six weeks.

1979: FIRST YEAR 2000 PARTY PLANS. Twenty students from Yale University formed the Millennium Society. Their goal: To throw the biggest party in history, on December 31, 1999. Today, they're still working on it (see page 2006).

1970

1975: FIRST YEAR 2000 SCOTCH. The Bushmills distillery in County Antrim, Ireland, distilled a special scotch for the year 2000 (see page 2067).

1987: FIRST COUNTDOWN CLOCK. In 1987, on the 10th anniversary of the opening of the Pompidou Centre in Paris, President François Mitterand inaugurated a countdown clock displaying the number of seconds left until the year 2000. "A nation must orient its gaze toward the future," Mitterand declared (see page 2099).

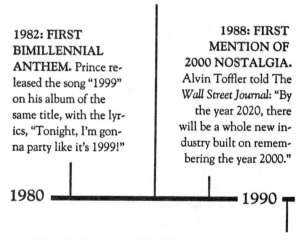

1982: FIRST BIMILLENNIAL ANTHEM. Prince released the song "1999" on his album of the same title, with the lyrics, "Tonight, I'm gonna party like it's 1999!"

1988: FIRST MENTION OF 2000 NOSTALGIA. Alvin Toffler told The *Wall Street Journal*: "By the year 2020, there will be a whole new industry built on remembering the year 2000."

1980

1990

1991: FIRST 2000 TRADEMARK. Mark Mitten, a former advertising executive in Chicago, registered the name Billennium (a combination of *bi* and *millennium*) with the U.S. Trademark Office. He was thus able to call his project "the official celebration of the year 2000."

1991: FIRST HUGE PRIVATE PARTY. After being turned down for six years, Wendy Warren of Portland, Oregon finally leased Seattle's Space Needle. For an undisclosed amount, Warren and 14 other families get exclusive use of the Needle beginning at 8 p.m., December 31, 1999. She plans a party with 900 guests.

1992: FIRST YEAR 2000 POLL. The Millennium Poll by Yankelovich Clancy Shulman finds that 59% expect to do the same old thing on New Year's Eve, 1999.

1994: FIRST HOTEL PROMOTION. The Sheraton Hotel in Phuket, Thailand ran a "Countdown 2000" promotional package to commemorate the fact that July 11, 1994 is 2000 days before the year 2000.

1995

1993: FIRST EMCEE. ABC-TV signed eternal teenager Dick Clark to host "New Year's Rockin' Eve" in Times Square on December 31, 1999.

1995: FIRST CALENDAR *The Millennium Planner* included the first-ever calendar for 2000...and incorrectly identified 2000 as the first year of the new millennium.

Collecting Debts in 1999:

ZAP! "OK, OK! I'LL..."
ZAP! "...PAY YOU!" ZAP!

Another outlandish glimpse of life in 1999 from Looking
Forward, *the 1903 novel by Arthur Bird (see page 2011).
Apparently, Bird believed electricity could solve every so-
cial problem—in this case, collecting outstanding debts.*

In 1899, the relations between creditor and debtor were not as cordial as they should be. [But that gradually changed.]

Beginning in 1930, creditors and debtors kept in closer electrical touch with one another. If the sum due was $50 or over and of long standing, the law allowed the creditor to connect his debtor with an electrical battery ....If the debt was over three months due, the creditor was allowed to occasionally "touch up" his debtor without having to hunt him up. The creditor always had him "on the string" so to speak.

It was further specified by law that creditors must employ only as many volts as there were dollars due on account in shocking a debtor. These electrical shocks were merely reminders, intended to refresh the memory of the debtor. A man owing

$200 was liable to receive two hundred volts until the debt was satisfied.

This plan for the collection of bad debts worked very successfully. In 1999 no debtor could tell when his creditor might touch him up. The shock reminding him of his old debt might come during the night and disturb his pleasant sleep. Perhaps while seated at the family table, or perhaps even while engaged in family worship, an electric shock might come that would raise him three feet off the floor.

Such little occurrences were rather embarrassing, especially if the debtor was talking at the time to some lady friend. A man owing $500 was in danger of his life. His creditor was liable to dun him by giving him a shock of five hundred volts. Such sensations, certainly, are not as pleasant as watching a yacht race, with your boat an easy winner.

A curious illustration of the operation of this new condition between creditors and bad debtors came to light in a parish church on the banks of the St. Lawrence. It appears that the village school teacher, who was busy with a Saturday evening rehearsal. The members of the choir were in their places, while the professor stood near the communion-rail, facing the choir, with his back turned towards the empty pews. He was speaking, when suddenly his red hair stood on end, his whiskers straightened out at right angles, while his eyes looked big as door knobs. He then gave a leap in the air, turned a somersault backwards and cleared ten pews before landing again on his feet. It appears that he owed his landlord an old board bill of $120 and the latter had just given him an electrical dun. The choir was astounded at the professor's performance. The latter excused himself and merely said it was a slight attack of the "grippe."

RANDOM THOUGHT

"Were I to choose an auspicious image for the new millennium, I would choose…the sudden agile leap of the poet-philosopher who raises himself above the weight of the world, showing that with all his gravity he has the secret of lightness, and that what many consider to be the vitality of the times—noisy, aggressive, revving and roaring—belongs to the realm of death, like a cemetery for rusty old cars."

—Italo Calvino,
Six Memos for the Next Millennium (1988)

Have we crashed yet?
THE COMPUTER BUG
Part 2

In Part I (page 2046), we filled in a little of the background on the Y2K problem. But the question you're probably asking is: What's going to happen?

H OW BAD IS IT?
No one is sure. Since so much of our society relies on computers, the effects of the problem could be huge. On the other hand, awareness of the problem is high and most businesses and organizations are working on a solution. Paul Saffo of the Institute for the Future calls the problem a "low-probablity, high-consequence event, " suggesting that "the most likely scenario by far is that we'll muddle through."

But consider this: In most mainframe programs the date appears about once every 50 lines of code. It's often hard to find those lines because the original programs were written in COBOL, an ancient computer language.

To fix the problem, programmers have to find the lines with date code in them, then rewrite them to recognize the correct date. Or they can use a program that does it for them. But then comes the most time-consuming step—testing the rewritten program. "It's an issue of magnitude, not of technical complexity, says Rick Cowles, a Y2K consultant.

Since the process can take so much time, even companies (and government agencies) that have been working on fixing the problem may not *finish* fixing the problem by the time 2000 arrives. "I think most of it will be fixed," says Edward Yardeni, chief economist at Deutsche Bank Securities. "But not all of it will be fixed. And those will have a domino effect."

PUT IT ON MY TAB

Not only is the solution time-consuming, it's expensive. The Federal Government is already spending billions to become "Y2K compliant" (i.e., making sure a system's vital functions will be operational in 2000). The IRS alone estimates they'll spend more than $1 billion.

Cost estimates for the private sector run as high as $600 billion—an amount that one report claims "could easily fund a year's worth of all US educational costs, preschool through grad school." And that's not counting legal costs, which some claim could top $1 trillion.

WHAT COULD HAPPEN?

So if everyone's systems aren't fixed by 2000, what happens? Scenarios range from the collapse of the civilized world to mild annoyance.

"Many software experts believe millions of computer systems [will] go haywire," writes Chris O' Malley in *Time*. "Shutting down life as we know it and turning our information age into a digitally dysfunctional society. Electric and phone service [could] be lost. Banks and supermarkets shuttered. Life savings [could] vanish and lives be imperiled."

Other experts expect satellites to fall from the sky, nuclear meltdowns, the failure of hospital life-support systems, and the collapse of the air-traffic system.

And still others warn of the impending legal problems Y2K will spawn—ranging from breach of warranty suits to fraud to management negligence suits. "It will be two to three times as big as the problem itself—and it will last longer," claims securities analyst Terrence Tierney. "Every lawyer in the world is lining up on this."

IT'S A SMALL WORLD

All of which doesn't even account for how the problem may affect us globally. Many of our systems are interdependent. So even if every system in the U.S. gets fixed in time, we still may be affected by problems in other countries.

In fact, some economists expect a global, yearlong recession which would also hit the U.S. "This year the American economy is a supertanker, but next year it is going to be Titanic America," claims one economist.

Much of the world *is* doing something to either fix or minimize the problem. European countries have formed governmental Y2K task forces. The government of Singapore has offered to help small and mid-size companies pay for Y2K repairs. An English parliament member has introduced a bill attempting to make it illegal for companies not to become Y2K compliant.

But the outlook is still mixed. A handful of countries seem to be taking little action, if any at all. Reports suggest that many African countries are far behind and that Russia is complacent about the problem. "As bad as it seems in the United States," writes *Newsweek*, "the rest of the world is lagging far behind."

TECHNO-HYPE?

Of course, not everyone is worried. Some feel that Y2K is mostly hype. "To be truthful," says Tom Giammo, a retired US Patent and Trade Office engineer, "I have grown somewhat skeptical that the year 2000 problem is really anything of this magnitude...Each of the groups who are technically capable of analyzing the problem seem to have a vested interest in exaggerating its size...and the media sells its products on bad news, not good news."

Some see it as just one more apocalyptic scenario, "I have spent a lot of time on the Web trying to make sense of Y2K hysteria, which seems more of a religious phenomenon than a technological one," says author Fred Moody.

"Not for 1,000 years or so has so much dread provoked, and so much money made, in preparation for something that will amount to so little."

One author suggests the "panic" is a set-up—that some high-tech firm is going to appear at the last minute with a "silver bullet" to solve the problem. "If you were Microsoft," he says, "and you had unlimited financial resources, what project would you invest in? What project would offer the best PR and financial return? Y2K. The smartest people in America will be working on this. The incentive is too powerful to ignore."

Others find those notions naive. "Hey, drug companies make money from heart medication," writes technical editor Edmund X. DeJesus. "Maybe heart disease is a hoax, too. Now is not the time to complain that the lifeboat builders are making money."

CULTURE SHOCK

Regardless of whether Y2K is hype or a real threat, the problem and its effects has captured our cultural imagination. In 1994, Y2K newsletter *Tick, Tick, Tick* held a worst-case scenario contest. The winner entered the following doomsday scenario:

"Let's suppose that the U.S. Department of Defense wrote a small program in the 1950s which still runs daily between the Pentagon and several missile silos out in the middle of Iowa. And let's suppose the purpose of the program is to compare the date of today's commands with the date of yesterday's commands.

"Now let's suppose further still through an act of espionage the former Soviet Union acquired the same technology, but that it operates daily between the Kremlin and missile silos in the Ukraine. If the dates and/or date logic are not century sensitive then the following test could put us all into big trouble on January 1st, 2000.

'If today's date is one day greater than yesterday's date, everything is okay. [Otherwise] assume a serious breach (eg. Headquarters has been destroyed) and fire the missiles toward the enemy.'"

APOCALYPSE NOT

While conceding the problem is bad, most experts aren't exactly expecting the end of the world. "These horror scenarios have a certain plausibility," says Federal Reserve Governor Edward Kelley . "[But] by no means is it baked in the cake that this is going to be a severe economic disruption or disaster."

"There will be some extremely annoying, disruptive failures," says Steven Hock, president of Triaxsys Research. "But it's not going to be the apocalypse."

Oops!
WHAT ABOUT
THE COMPUTER?

As Y2K becomes more important, you may find yourself
wondering how futurists—whose specialty is anticipating
trends and technology—could have overlooked
such an obvious problem. The truth is, they
missed much more than that.

NO CRYSTAL BALL

Experts have made many impressive predictions over the last century. But when it comes to personal computers, they generally goofed. In fact, the home computer revolution is frequently cited as *the* example of the failure of futurology. From the late writings of H. G. Wells to the early writings of Alvin Toffler, the significance of computers in our homes was almost always overlooked.

TYPICAL ATTITUDES

One reason: the revolution took place so quickly that hardly anyone understood its significance. "The computer as defined today did not exist in 1950," Paul Ceruzzi notes in his 1986 book, *Imagining Tomorrow*. "Before World War II, the word *computer* meant a human being who worked at a desk with a calculating machine."

Even people who worked with computers tended to downplay their importance:

"I think there's a world market for maybe five computers."
> —Thomas Watson, chairman of IBM, 1943

"I have traveled the length and breadth of this country and talked with the best people, and I can assure you that data-processing is a fad that won't last out the year."
> —Business book editor, Prentice-Hall, 1957

"There is no reason anyone would want a computer in their home."
> —Ken Olson, president and founder,
> Digital Equipment Corporation, 1977

Even as computers gained acceptance, official estimates of the growth of the industry were consistently off the mark. "Computers are multiplying at a rapid rate," the *Wall Street Journal* wrote in 1966. "By the turn of the century, there will be 220,000 in the U.S."

Undoubtedly, that sounded like a radical prediction at the time—after all, only 10 years earlier there had been fewer than *1,000* computers in the U.S. But it was ludicrously conservative—today there are millions.

The fact that virtually everyone failed to anticipate the most important technological innovation of our generation—and perhaps the entire century—is food for thought: something to remember when *we* ponder what may happen in the future.

$ Cashing in on 2000 $

TAKE THE
MONEY AND RUN

*It was true in 1000 A.D. and it's true today: people
will do almost anything for money. So read the fine
print before you buy millennium merchandise,
or you might wind up with junk like...*

REAGANBUSH TREE SEEDS Liberty Tree
Corp. offered these seeds in the 1980s with a promise that a register of the names, addresses, and tree numbers of all Reaganbush owners would be "presented" to the National Archives in the year 2000.

Fine Print: It turns out that the National Archives doesn't accept private documents—only federal government records.

THE MILLENNIUM YEARBOOK A publication created by a group calling itself "Gift to the Future 2000." Participants contribute their words of wisdom...which are guaranteed to be published in a hardbound book. "Hundreds of years from now," the company's brochure reads, "...we foresee the sociologists and philosophers of future generations poring over these manuscripts...to learn what we as peoples felt and thought."

Fine Print: It's a grand idea, but surprise! You have to pay money to participate. And if you read the offer carefully, you'll notice that by signing the consent form, you assign the company "all copyright" of your personal statement—so it can be, in their words, "published in other books, publications and commercial advertisement" without your consent.

* * *

SPACE PATROL

"In the year 2000, we on this Earth will have visited new worlds."
—**President Richard Nixon, July 21, 1969**

"I don't think we should be too timid to say that at the end of the century, we're going to put a man on Mars; somebody's going to do it."
—**Vice President Spiro T. Agnew, July 16, 1969**

"By the year 2000, we will undoubtedly have a sizeable operation on the moon; we will have achieved a manned Mars landing; and it's entirely possible we will have flown with men to the outer planets."
—**Werner von Braun, NASA scientist, 1969**

Good News!
THE SPACE BROTHERS
👽 ARE COMING! 👽

Here's a thought: Maybe aliens in UFOs really have been watching us. Maybe they know that the year 2000 is the precise time they're expected to show up. That might explain why people like Ruth Norman seem so certain they'll be joining us at the party.

THE FAIRY QUEEN

Ruth Norman, "grand dame of the New Age," became famous in the 1980s by appearing regularly on cable access TV in San Diego, dressed as a fairy godmother. She called herself "Space Fleet Commander."

Norman could hardly wait for the new millennium because, she explained, that's when the "Space Brothers" would finally arrive.

THE SPACE BROTHERS

As the leader of UNARIUS (Universal Articulate Interdimensional Understanding of Science), it was her job to spread the news that a fleet of 33 interlocking spaceships, each carrying 1,000 Space Brothers, would land in the year 2001 and deliver a message of peace to the world.

Norman worked hard at it. She wrote dozens of books about the Space Brothers. And in 1975 she purchased 73 acres of land in southeastern San Diego County so they'd have a good place to land.

THE SUNNY SIDE OF THE STREET

Norman's vision for the new millennium was relentlessly optimistic. "The arrival of extraterrestrials in 2001 will signal the real beginning of the Age of Logic and Reason, and the *Renaissance of Spirit* of mankind," she declared. And she wrote: "Man's destiny is infinite in nature, or if you prefer to call it, godlike! ...This will be [apparent] when man begins to seek answers through the science We Space Brothers have brought to Earth!"

PAST AND FUTURE

Norman and her Unarian followers believed in reincarnation. She claimed she had been, among others, Mary Magdalene, Socrates, Buddha, and King Arthur. She also maintained that her late husband had been the reincarnation of Jesus. Her nickname, URIEL (Universal, Radiant, Infinite, Eternal Light) combined traits of all her incarnations.

URIEL expected to live until 2001. ("The spaceships," she told The *Los Angeles Times*, "I wouldn't miss those for the world.") But she passed into "the next universe" at the age of 92, in 1993. Maybe she'll be back in time.

For More On UNARIUS: www.serve.com/unarius/

Millennium Geography
WHERE DOES 2000 START?
Part I

*You may not know it, but there's some confusion
about where the new millennium will officially start
—is it in England or in the South Pacific? The debate
goes back to 1884, when the International Dateline
was created. Tip: You may have to read this chapter
two or three times before it makes any sense.*

T HE PRIME MERIDIAN
   In 1884, an international conference (see page
2052) decided that the meridian (longitude line) running
through Greenwich, England, would be the "prime meridian." That means the *official* day for the world—called the
Universal Day—starts there.

The conference also decided that the meridian exactly
opposite Greenwich (on the other side of the globe, in the
South Pacific) would be the International Dateline—
where the *actual* day for the world starts.

CONFUSING SITUATION

This created a confusing situation. How can we have two
different places where the day starts?

The answer: One spot is for keeping track of international time; the other is there because…well…the sun has to come up *somewhere* first.

Why didn't the conference just designate Greenwich as the spot where the sun comes up first? Because Greenwich Mean Time (GMT) is the *average* time for the world; it has to be positioned halfway between the first and last light of the day. Thus, when it's midnight in Greenwich, it's already noon at the dateline in the South Pacific.

Most of us would probably conclude that this is nonsense—the day starts where the sun comes up. But the Greenwich folks (and international law) disagree.

The result is that there are two general areas claiming to be the place where 2000 begins. "There are people going crazy to know…whether the millennium will start on the International Dateline [or on the Greenwich Meridian]," says one expert. But there's no definitive answer.

SO WHICH IS IT?

If you understand all this, you can come up with your own opinion. For the record, the official position is that people who live in the South Pacific, along the International Dateline, move into the year 2000 first…but "only in local time, measured relative to GMT." Meanwhile, the debate continues. *And there's more to the story; for Part II, turn to page 2181*

Predictions from the Past
"IN 2000, YOUR HOME WILL FLY!"

*What?! You still use a vacuum cleaner? Your TV
doesn't cook? What century are you living in,
anyway? Didn't anyone ever tell you that
by now we're supposed to have...*

MIGRATING HOUSES

"[Using] wonderful new materials far stronger
than steel, but lighter than aluminum...houses [in the
year 2001] will be able to fly....The time may come when
whole communities may migrate south
in the winter, or move to new lands
whenever they feel the need for a
change of scenery."

> —Arthur C. Clarke,
> "The World of 2001,"
> *Vogue* magazine, 1966

TV-OVENS

"In the year 2000, we will live in pre-fabricated houses
light enough for two men to assemble...[We'll] cook in

our television sets and relax in chairs that emit a private
sound-light-color spectacular."

—The *New York Times*, January 7, 1968

ULTRASONIC CLEANERS

"Keeping house will be a breeze by the year 2000. Sonic
cleaning devices and air-filtering systems will just about
eliminate dusting, scrubbing and vacuuming. There may
be vibrating floor grills by doors to clean shoes, and elec-
trostatic filters will be installed in entrances to remove
dust from clothes with ultrasonic waves."

—Staff of The *Wall Street Journal*,
*Here Comes Tomorrow! Living and
Working in the Year 2000*, (1966)

WATERPROOF FURNITURE

"When [the housewife of 2000] cleans house she simply
turns the hose on everything. Why not? Furniture—(up-
holstery included), rugs, draperies, unscratchable floors—
all are made of synthetic fabric or waterproof plastic.
After the water has run down a drain in the middle of
the floor (later concealed by a rug of synthetic fiber),
[she] turns on a blast of hot air and dries everything."

—Waldemarr Kaempffert,
Popular Mechanics, (1950)

DISH-MAKERS

"Dishwashing will be a thing of the past [in 2000]. Disposable dishes will be made from powdered plastic for each meal by a machine in the kitchen....With a brand-new 'dishmodeling machine,' disposable plates, bowls and cups can be made for a few pennies a meal."

—The Philco Corporation, (1967)

DISSOLVING DISHES

"Housewives in 50 years may wash dirty dishes right down the drain. Cheap plastic [will] melt in hot water."

—*Popular Mechanics*, (1950)

*   *   *

THINKING ABOUT THE FUTURE

"Today there are over 5 billion humans on the planet, and more are on the way. Each person has the potential to create and share with the world an idea or invention that will change the course of history.

"However, this will not happen unless we encourage our children, who are the people of the next millennium, to think expansively and offer their thoughts to others."

—Isaac Asimov

$ Cashing in on 2000 $
THE "NAME GAME"

*For generations, companies tacked "2000"
onto products whenever they wanted to give the
impression something was trendy and up-to-date.
Now there are thousands of brand names that
may have to be changed. For example…*

ET 2000: Exercise trainers

Max 2000: Automatic hand-dryer

Bic 2000: Disposable lighter

Mega-2000: Vitamin product

Easy Care 2000: Adjustable bed

Impact 2000: Door jambs, moldings

Face-Shade 2000: Car windowshades

Huntmaster-2000: Archery-arrow rests

RU 2000: Gasoline

Powerplak 2000: Electric toothbrush

Circa 2000: Wall coverings

Klip-2000: Racket strings

Vodocoder 2000: Musical synthesizers

T2000: Baseball glove

Compliance 2000: IRS campaign

Contract 2000: Carpets and rugs

Vega 2000: Airbrush

Computron 2000: Digital watches

Uncle John's
HANDY GUIDE TO THE END OF THE WORLD
Part II

Here are more "end-time" predictions—this time from three Native American sources.

HOPI

Background: A Pueblo tribe that today occupies several mesa villages in northeast Arizona. Their stories are passed on orally. Frankly, if they are really from ancient times, and not "backdated" by someone to make them sound more accurate, they're pretty amazing.

Signs the End Is Near: According to many Hopi tribal elders (such as Dan Evehama, Thomas Banyacya, and Martin Gashwaseoma), the coming of "white-skinned men" and "a strange beast, like a buffalo but with great long horns" that would "overrun the land" (cattle) were predicted as precursors to the end of time. They also say their prophecies include:

• "The land will be crossed by snakes of iron and rivers of stone. The land shall be criss-crossed by a giant spider's web. Seas will turn black."

• "A great dwelling-place in the heavens shall fall with a

great crash. It will appear as a blue star. The world will rock to and fro."

• "The white man will battle people in other lands, with those who possess the first light of wisdom. Terrible will be the result. There will be many columns of smoke in the deserts. These are the signs that great destruction is here."

When the World Ends: Many will die, but those "who understand the prophecies...and stay and live in the places of my people (Hopi) shall also be safe."

• Pahana, the True White Brother will return to plant the seeds of wisdom in people's hearts and usher in the dawn of the Fifth World.

For More On the Hopi: www.timesoft.com/hopi/

MAYANS

Background: An ancient Meso-American civilization with a highly developed, extraordinarily accurate system of mathematics and astronomy. Many people think the Mayan calendar ends at around 2012 or 2013, and assume that's the scheduled date for the end of the world.

Signs the End Is Near: According to *The Mayan Prophecies*, the earth will be destroyed by environmental disasters—earthquakes, tidal waves, you name it. Civilization will collapse; then Kulkulcan (Quetzalcoatl)—a feathered serpent deity who represents the forces of good and light—will arrive.

When the World Ends: Again, according to *The Mayan Prophecies*: "The end of artificial time signals...the return to natural time, a time in harmony with the Earth and with the natural cycles....It holds within it the potential to reinstate a balanced, positive love and unity."

For More On the Mayans: www.halfmoon.org/

SIOUX

Background: A confederation of several Native American Plains tribes. They also have an oral tradition.

Signs the End Is Near: According to an Ogalala (Sioux) medicine man, a "darkness descends over the tribe...the world is out of balance. There are floods, fires and earthquakes. There is a great drought." A White Buffalo will be born and the White Buffalo Calf Woman (according to legend, a representative of the spirit world) will return.

When the World Ends: White Buffalo Calf Woman will purify the world. "She will bring back harmony again, and balance, spiritually."

Note: A white buffalo was born in 1994...and another in 1995. Many tribal elders feel these are clear signs that their prophecy is being fulfilled. "Yes indeed, it is a sign," says one. "The important ones are the last two. These were created with the influence of the Masters."

For More On the Sioux: www.blackhills-info.com/lakota_sioux/

Whatever Happened to...
ROBOTS

*People were once sure that by the year 2000, robots would
be doing our household chores. "Robots are coming—
not to rule the world but to help around the house,"
promised Walter Cronkite in a 1967 TV
show. Well...where are they?*

BACKGROUND
The concept of robots is old, but the word isn't. It
was introduced in Karel Capek's 1921 play *R.U.R.*
(comes from the Czech word *robota*, which means
"work").

R.U.R. (or *Rossum's Universal Robots*) depicts a society
where robots did all the dirty work—sweeping streets, laying bricks, manufacturing and farming. Female robots per-
formed secretarial duties.

"All work will be done by living machines," the General Manager of R.U.R. explains in one scene. "Everybody
will be free from worry and liberated from the degradation
of labor. Everybody will live only to perfect himself."

AN IDEA WHOSE TIME HAS COME
In the 1960s, the Space Race provided the impetus and

funding for the development of sophisticated robotics. It seemed reasonable that by 2000, mechanical helpers like the Jetsons' Rosie the Robot would be commonplace.

- "Machines like these may help cook your breakfast and serve it, too…We may wake up each morning to the patter of little feet—robot feet."

—Walter Cronkite, *Life in 2001*, (1967)

- "By the year 2000, housewives…will probably have a robot "maid'…shaped like a box (with one large eye on the top, several arms and hands, and long narrow pads on the side for moving about."

—The *New York Times*, July 12, 1966

- "We shall face the novel sensation of trying to determine whether the smiling, assured humanoid behind the airline reservation counter is a pretty girl or a carefully wired robot."

—Alvin Toffler,
Future Shock, (1970)

BUT NOT YET

Twenty years later, the space program was on the rocks… and many futurologists changed their minds. There would be no domestic helper like Rosie.

- "A robot that cooks, cleans and irons shirts isn't even on the drawing board," wrote The *Chicago Tribune*. "The all-purpose automated maid of 'The Jetsons' TV series is still a wistful dream."

• "The domestic robot simply won't be able to do enough meaningful chores around the house to be cost effective. Who's going to pay $25,000 for a robot that dusts, mops and vacuums but can't do windows?"

—Marvin Cetron and Thomas J. O'Toole,
Encounters with the Future, (1982)

SO, WHEN?

Now we're almost to 2000—and where are the robots? It seems that the skeptics were right...except...maybe the robots are ready, but we're not. On April 30, 1998, the *Christian Science Monitor* wrote:

According to many robot scientists...latent mistrust of robots is a pervasive cultural problem. As robotics and intelligent machines are poised now with amazing possibilities to transform daily life, the bump in the road to acceptance is not technology. Just as personal computers were not embraced by the general public some 20-years ago, robots...are up against old-fashioned resistance to change.

They offered a case history:

Mark Tilden, a laboratory scientist, loves solar-powered robots. He invents them...and silently they clean floors, kill flies, and do kitchen chores. [But] "When my mother comes to visit," he says, "I have to put the robots away. She's afraid they will attack her in the middle of the night."

Nonetheless, robots are here to stay. According to the *Monitor*:

- "The Robotics Industries Association (RIA) in Ann Arbor, Mich., reports record sales of industrial strength robots—$1.1 billion in 1997, up 136% since 1992."
- "In Sacramento, Calif., a Shell gas station is experimenting with a robotic arm that opens a car's gas cap and fills the tank with gas."
- "In Japan, the RoboShop Super 24 uses robots exclusively to deliver selected food items to customers."
- "Nearly 100 hospitals across the country use Helpmate Robots, which deliver meals to patients, medical records to personnel, and supplies around the hospital."
- "There's a robot baby doll being developed that looks uncannily like a real child. A major U.S. toy manufacturer is looking into marketing them in 2000 or 2001."

Who knows? Maybe Rosie is next.

For More On Robots: www.ljkamm.com/robots.htm

Celebrity Psychic
THE GREAT CRISWELL

Here's a look at 2000 from our
all-time favorite psychic.

BACKGROUND

Although he's best known for his
cameo appearance in the worst movie
of all time—*Plan Nine from Outer
Space*—Jeron Criswell was also a
famous (or infamous) psychic. In 1968
he wrote *Criswell Predicts—From Now
to the Year 2000*, which has become a classic
of millennial weirdness. Criswell claims his predictions
have an 86% accuracy. "Over the next thirty years," he
tells readers, "you may keep your own score as to their
accuracy. After that, it will not matter." Here are some
of our favorite Criswell predictions:

APHRODISIAC SPRAY

"I predict that our own United States will, in the future,
be swept by the popular clouds of an Aphrodisian fra-
grance. It will be invented by a scientist who is searching
for an improved antiseptic spray. Instead he will invent a
spray that is almost odorless but when breathed stimulates
the most basic sexual erotic areas.

"This aroma will fill every man and woman who inhales it with uncontrollable passion...I predict that the sex urge will advance rapidly, and many men will flagrantly expose themselves in public. I predict a wealthy San Francisco attorney will announce his marriage to his mother and a Hollywood producer will openly declare his daughter is going to bear his child; a young man in Arkansas will ask to be legally wed to his pet cat."

BIRTH CONTROL

"I predict that birth control will no longer be a major problem in the United States. Placed in the water system of the country, in every city, regardless of size, will be chemicals which will act as contraceptives on the entire populace. In addition to this, the electricity that comes into each home will have certain ionic particles that cause contraception."

THE DESTRUCTION OF DENVER

"I predict that a large city in Colorado will be the victim of a strange and terrible pressure from outer space, which will cause all solids to turn into a jelly-like mass."

CANNIBALISM

"I predict an outburst of cannibalism that will terrorize the population of one of the industrial cities in the state of Pennsylvania—Pittsburgh!... I predict that over one thousand flesh-mad and blood-crazed men will wander the streets, suddenly attacking unsuspecting victims."

THE END!

"The world as we know it will cease to exist, as I have stated previously in this volume, on August 18, 1999.

"A study of all the prophets—Nostradamus, St. Odile, Mother Shipton, the Bible—indicates that we will cease to exist before the year 2000! Not one of these prophets even took the trouble to predict beyond the year 2000! And if you and I meet each other on the street that fateful day, August 18, 1999, and we chat about what we will do on the morrow, we will open our mouths to speak and no words will come out, for we have no future...you and I will suddenly run out of time! Who knows but what future generation from some other planet will dig down through seven layers of rubble and find us some 2,000 years hence, and crowd around a museum glass containing a broken fragment of a Coca Cola bottle, a bent hairpin and a parched copy of our Bible which managed to escape the terrifying destruction of our civilization! They will wonder what on earth was meant by the words 'Henry Ford' or 'Hollywood'...and what in heaven's name was a *Criswell*!"

WANT TO KNOW MORE ABOUT CRISWELL?
Contact: ourworld.compuserve.com/homepages/
andy_crickett/

Uncle John's
HANDY GUIDE TO THE PROPHETS OF DOOM #3

Here's our third installment of the Prophets of Doom (see page 2092 for #2). It's the group we call the "Pole People."

RICHARD KEININGER

Background: Keininger became a cult figure in 1962 after publishing *The Ultimate Frontier*, one of the best-selling underground books in the U.S. It describes the teachings of ancient mystic brotherhoods, supposedly passed on to Keininger by modern-day members.

His book was the first to place importance on the date May 5, 2000. That's the day a "planetary alignment" will occur. Five planets in our solar system—Mercury, Venus, Mars, Jupiter, and Saturn—will align themselves with Earth. (The six planets will form a line, with Earth at one end and Saturn at the other. The sun will sit between Earth and the other five.)

Doomsday 2000: Keininger believes that the planetary alignment will cause the poles to shift, causing a host of cataclysmic changes on earth. Seismic activity will increase. The continental arches will buckle. Carbon

2167

dioxide and sulfur dioxide will be released by volcanic eruption. Hurricanes and tsunami will rage across large parts of the earth. Dust and fumes will blot out the sun for months. Animals and vegetation will be shredded into muck. The stench of decay and destruction will cover the earth…and people who survive will be driven insane by the carnage. All won't be lost, however. Those who have "the strength of their convictions" will live to see the formation of the Kingdom of God soon after October, 2001.

Believability Factor: See next page.

JEFFREY GOODMAN AND RICHARD NOONE

Background: The two are not connected as far as we know, except in their belief that May 5, 2000 is doomsday. Dr. Goodman wrote *We Are the Earthquake Generation* (1978); Noone wrote the cult classic *5 / 5 / 2000* (1982).

Doomsday 2000: They, too, claim that magnetic waves will create a pole shift, causing earthquakes, floods, and giant tsunami. "On that day," Richard Noone writes, "the ice build-up at the South Pole will upset the earth's axis—sending trillions of tons of ice and water sweeping over the surface of our planet."

Goodman predicts this scene: "Giddiness is induced from subtle gravitational and magnetic changes that the earth's shifting in space is creating….The sky reddens as huge clouds begin to blot out the sun...Quakes and volcanoes are set off around the world and a rift opens up as the earth splits in several places to relieve the stress produced by the shift...Then material from the sky starts to come crashing down." In the end, much of humanity is wiped out.

Believability Factor: How realistic is this scenario? In 1994, a worried reader asked Joel Achenbach, who writes a column for The *Washington Post* called "Why Things Are." Achenbach replied that "planetary alignments" are a sham because "the planets don't really line up." And even if the planets were perfectly aligned—which is virtually impossible—the effect would generate only a .0001 change in the tidal force on earth.

An astronomer explains: "The absolute gravitational force from another body in space isn't really that important. It's the tidal force that makes a difference. In fact, with the planets in the position they will be in on the big day, the largest tidal force from one of them will be from Jupiter, and it is about one five hundred thousandth the size of the tidal force exerted by the moon on an average day." Still, if civilization survives Nostradamus, George Washington, Y2K, etc., you can bet millions of people will be holding their breath on 5 / 5 / 2000.

Still want more? See Prophets of Doom #4 on Page 2200

![2000]

Be in Two Centuries at Once!
THE ULTIMATE
2000 PARTY STUNT

Still looking for a place to spend New Year's Eve?
How about booking a cruise? You could literally
end up with one foot in each century.

Here's an interesting way to spend December 31, 1999: Reserve space on a ship that's anchored in the Pacific, straddling the International Dateline. Then you'll be able to walk forward into a new century... or stroll back to the old one.

There's an historical precedent for this stunt. The story was told in *The Pointer*—a newsletter put out by U.S. Navy Armed Guard WWII veterans.

THE *SS WARRIMOO*

"The night was warm and inviting, and the stars shone in all their tropical brilliance. Captain John D. S. Phillips was in a dark corner of the bridge, quietly pulling on a cigar with all the contentment that comes to a sailor when he knows the voyage is half completed.

"His ship, the passenger steamer *SS Warrimoo*, was quietly knifing her way through the waters of the mid-Pacific on her way from Vancouver to Australia. The navigator had just finished working out a star fix and brought Capt. Phillips the results. The ship, it seemed, was spotted at latitude zero degrees–30 minutes north and longitude 179–30 minutes west. The date was Dec. 30, 1899.

"What this meant, of course, was that the *Warrimoo* was only a few miles from the intersection of the equator and the International Dateline.

AN HISTORIC PRANK

"Captain Phillips double-checked the position of his ship with four additional navigators. They confirmed the ship's exact position. Then Captain Phillips, a prankish fellow, changed course slightly and made for the intersection of the dateline and the equator. He adjusted the ship's speed to arrive at exactly the right time.

"The calm weather, the clear night and the eager cooperation of his entire crew worked successfully in the captain's favor. At precisely midnight, local time, the *Warrimoo* lay exactly on the equator at exactly the point where it crosses the International Dateline!

"The consequences of this bizarre position were many. The forward part of the ship was in the Southern Hemisphere and in the middle of summer. The stern was in the Northern Hemisphere and in the middle of winter. The date in the after-part of the ship was Dec. 30, 1899. Forward, it was [Dec. 31, and then, at midnight,] Jan. 1, 1900.

"The ship was therefore not only in two different days, two different months, two different seasons and two different years, but in two different centuries [Ed. note: Well, not really]—all at the same time. Moreover, [as the boat steamed on,] the passengers were cheated out of a New Year's Eve celebration, and an entire day—Dec. 31, 1899—disappeared from their lives for all time.

"There were compensations, however, for the people aboard the *Warrimoo* were undoubtedly the first to greet the new century. Capt. Phillips, speaking of the event years later, said 'I never heard of it happening before, and I guess it won't happen again until the year 2000!'"

MILLENNIUM CRUISES

He was right. In fact, most of the world's cruise lines have already made plans to sail to the International Dateline for New Year's Eve. For instance:

• The Millennium First Sail Organization plans to bring more than 2000 boats there.

• Silversea Cruises has sister ships that will cross the Dateline for their *Millennium 2000 Celebration* voyage.

• Crystal Cruises has two millennium cruises to the Dateline (both are sold out).

If you're interested, but can't find an open berth for 2000...well, you can always book a cruise in time for the *real* millennium—January 1, 2001.

More Predictions from the Past
"YOUR CLOTHES WILL BE SOLAR-POWERED IN 2000."

*Imagine yourself lounging around in 2000. What will
you be wearing: a paper dress...a glow-in-the-dark
loincloth...or the same old blue jeans and T-shirt?
In 1981, author Lucille Khornak asked fashion
designers to take a guess. Here are some of their
answers from Khornak's book* Fashion 2001:

SOLAR-POWERED CLOTHES

"Solar power packs, which will be designed into the
shoulders of the garment, will draw energy from the sun
and store it. Tubes to distribute this energy will extend
from the shoulders through the entire suit. The retentive
fibers will heat in the winter and cool in the summer by
means of a control system."

—Larry Le Gaspi

DISPOSABLE CLOTHING

"A superb paper throwaway dress...will have all the tex-
ture and quality of silk or cotton. The elite will wear limited editions of paper dresses signed by the most outstanding artists of the time."

—Mary McFadden

PUSH-BUTTON WARDROBE

"We will press a button to formulate our clothing....Do we want it to be opaque, should it give off steam, do we want it to light up, do we want it to sparkle or do we prefer a matte finish, do we want it to glow in the dark?"

—Betsy Johnson

LOIN-CLOTHS

"In our own homes we will wear only the essentials; we will be Tarzan and Jane in a cushioned, caressing jungle."

—Chevali

FORMAL ATTIRE

"I envision a woman in a vaporous dress, entering a spatial gray-and-black Rolls-Royce which will cross the universe for a party on Venus, where all the men will be dressed in black tie."

—Jean-Baptiste Caumont

COLORED SKIN

"In the year 2001, a person will be able to change the color of his skin at will."

—Louis Feraud

THE SAME OLD STUFF

"We will never lose the nostalgia for another era. By the year 2001, people may be nostalgic for the eighties."

—Bill Blass

Science Fiction from 1903
MEET THE MUGLUGS

The word "robot" hadn't been coined in 1903, when William Wallace Cook wrote his novel, A Round Trip to the Year 2000—so he called his mechanical men "muglugs." In this excerpt Lumley, the hero from 1900, has his first encounter with a muglug in 2000.

Lumley fell asleep. He did not awake for several hours. When he again opened his eyes he found himself in a gorgeous chamber replete with luxurious furnishing. The bed on which he lay did not differ greatly from the 1900 beds which he had known, except that it was infinitely softer.

It had a massive canopy of purple silk. At the foot there was a silver button, with the words:

"Press Button When Ready to Get Up."

Lumley pressed one foot against the button.

Instantly a carved door shot open, admitting a dapper little muglug with gloved hands and rubber-shod feet. Gliding straight to the bed, it plucked Lumley from his bed, carried him to a lavatory, and dipped him in a perfumed bath. The drying was not by towels, but by a draft of hot air.

Lumley was then hustled into a warm robe, seated comfortably, and shaved with an electric machine that did the work thoroughly in less than two seconds. Next, his hair was dressed, and immediately after that the muglug tried to put him into a pair of bloomers [Ed. note: loose-fitting pants, worn only by women at the time], but Lumley rebelled and called for help.

"What's up?" asked the voice of Tibilus through the thought machine.

"I want my own clothes," answered Lumley.

Tibilus laughed till he almost cracked the transmitter. "Give him his own suit, mug," he said finally.

In a few minutes Lumley was decked out in his 1900 clothes. They were worn and shiny, a button was gone here and there ...but they were a hundred times better than bloomers.

Lumley found Tibilus in the newsroom, listening to the latest domestic transmissions.

"Greetings, friend Lumley," said Tibilus. "How do you like being dressed by machinery?"

"The year 2000 is not just a new century, but a religious experience." —**John Naisbitt**

2176

Important Influence #5
2001: A SPACE ODYSSEY

*In 1994, the Film Society of Lincoln Center noted:
"Few filmmakers can claim, with any credibility, to
have changed the way we look at movies. Fewer still
can claim to have changed the way we look at the
world. With 2001: A Space Odyssey, Stanley
Kubrick achieved both."*

CLAIM TO FAME This movie gave the millennium a name, a theme song ("Thus Spake Zarathustra"), and an intellectual presence in pop culture.

2001 presented the millennium as a philosophical challenge, explains the *Houston Chronicle*. "It's not about prophecies, but about possibilities. And it doesn't offer answers, but questions…It mixes glorious futurism with a daunting view of our tiny place in the universe."

BACKGROUND In 1964, after he'd finished making *Dr. Stangelove*, director Stanley Kubrick approached futurologist Arthur Clarke with a sketchy idea about making a special science fiction movie.

Kubrick explained that he wanted to explore the impact that the discovery of extra-terrestrial life would have on humankind. "Stanley was determined to create a work of art which would arouse the emotions of wonder, awe, even, if appropriate, terror," Clarke recalls.

Clarke, it turns out, had already addressed the subject of extra-terrestrial life in a 1948 short story called "The Sentinel." The plot device of the discovery of a monolith on the moon was eventually adapted from the story.

It took two years for Clarke and Kubrick to write the movie script. "We set out with the deliberate intention of creating a myth," says Clarke. "The Odyssean parallel was in our minds from the beginning, long before the film's title was chosen."

The title was chosen by Kubrick. (The film began production in 1966, when 2001 was still 35 years away.) Two years and $10.5 million dollars later, *2001: A Space Odyssey* was released—along with Clarke's novel of the same title, which went on to become one of the bestselling science-fiction books of all time.

IMPACT THEN "It now requires an effort of will," writes the Film Society of Lincoln Center, "to recapture the sense of shock and discovery that attended the film's initial release....Viewers felt they were 'standing' where no humans had ever stood before."

Nonetheless, many reviews were extremely negative. In The *New Yorker*, Pauline Kael called *2001* a "monumentally unimaginative movie." In The *Village Voice*, Andrew Sarris said it was "a disaster."

Eventually, however, most critics recognized *2001* as a milestone. One decided it was "the first truly intellectual epic in film history." Another belatedly credited it with "turning science fiction from a maligned realm of bug-eyed monsters into an artful, respected genre."

It was clear that *2001* had worked its way into pop culture when Elvis began using "Thus Spake Zarathustra" as the introduction to his concerts in the 1970s.

2001 and NASA: The film's most interesting impact was on NASA. "Released at the height of the…moon landing program," writes Russell Evansen in The *Wisconsin State Journal*, "*2001* seemed to embody the nation's space-crazy state of mind, and it fired the collective imaginations of all those who dreamed that one day humans would… light out for the stars." Everyone, from NASA technicians to astronauts, was captivated by it. Neil Armstrong watched it before heading for the moon. William Anders, one of the first humans to see the dark side of the moon (with Apollo 8), admitted he nearly radioed back to Mission Control that he'd just seen a monolith sailing by. (Clarke said he'd never forgive Anders for not doing it.) Even Alexei Leonov, the Russian cosmonaut who conducted the first spacewalk, told Clarke after viewing the film: "Now I feel I've been in space twice."

IMPACT NOW "*2001* still retains its power to awe and captivate," says Russell Evansen. "It has appeared on more lists of 'Ten Best Movies of All Time' than almost any other movie save *Citizen Kane*."

Elements from the film have entered the pop vernacular: the voice of the computer HAL, the mysterious black monolith, the StarChild, and, of course, the theme song are all still used in advertising today.

A High Standard. *2001* has become a standard by which we measure our progress. "Think of what we've missed," wrote Bruce Handy in The *New York Times* magazine in 1994. "If the movie *2001: A Space Odyssey* is to be believed, we could have had moon bases almost by now—not to mention astronauts who turn into giant translucent space fetuses."

"Undoubtedly, a favorite sport of the real year 2001 will be to dissect the film *2001* to see what has come true and what has not," suggests futurist Eric Lefcowitz. Some *2001* technology is already in use—e.g., the VideoPhone and high-security voice-ID systems. And though no artificial intelligence like HAL exists yet, "he" is the common reference point for practically everyone in the field. They all agree it's just a matter of time.

For More On 2001: www.Lehigh.EDU/~pjl2/kubrick/films/2001/

Fact or Fiction?
WHAT REALLY HAPPENED IN 1000 A.D.?, Part II

On page 2040, we told you the dramatic
tale of the "panic-terror" of 1000.
Here's the rest of the story.

W AS THERE REALLY A PANIC?

To put it simply, many historians think the story we quoted on page 2040 is nonsense.

"Students are always asking me, 'Ooh, what's going to happen in 2000?,'" says Norman Cohn, an expert on millenarian movements. "And I say there's no reason anything special should happen. The year 1000 was particularly quiet, as it happens."

MAYBE YES, MAYBE NO

Historical records from 1000 A.D. are pretty slim—and there's still debate about what happened. But in our opinion, the skeptics are probably right. A few reasons:

☞ There's no mention of millennial fears in any official documents of A.D. 1000—or in connection with any important events, such as the eruption of Mt. Vesuvius in 993 or Pope Gregory's death in 999.

☞ "The year 1000 sounds impressive," says *The Book of Predictions*, but in the Middle Ages, people used Roman numerals. It would simply have been "M" with no magic properties attached to it. Furthermore, numerical dates had little meaning to medieval people. Their lives were guided by the feast and fast days of the church, not calendars."

☞ The "panic-terror" story implies that Europeans all used the Common Calendar and celebrated New Year's on the same day. They didn't. There were dozens of different systems in use.

On top of that, there were no printed calendars, and no mechanical clocks. Given these conditions, the idea that the masses rose as one and embraced the terror is a little hard to swallow.

ORIGIN OF THE MYTH

So where did the tale come from? Probably a book called *Five Histories*, written in 1044 by a monk named Raoul Glaber. His account of the panic-terror is compelling enough to be believable...but it was written after the fact, and there's little evidence to support it.

The story really took hold in 18th-century France. According to *The Book of Predictions*: "Wishing to discredit the [values of] the Middle Ages, many writers such as Voltaire and Gibbon exaggerated the superstitions and credulous nature of medieval Christians." Anti-Catholic politicians also used it for their own purposes, "spreading the rumor that priests had used the millennium to defraud people of their land and money." Since then, it has been embellished and retold by dozens of modern authors.

THE MIDDLE GROUND

If there *was* a panic, it was probably confined to a few local areas. Henri Foucillon, a respected scholar, suggests that there were "stirrings in France, Lorraine, and Thuringia, toward the middle of the 10th century."

And maybe there were. But the interesting question is: Why do some people believe the story today?

HIGH ANXIETY

According to Peter N. Stearns in his book *Millennium III*, the reason is simple: anxiety about the millennium… which may not be a bad thing, if it "pushes people toward soul-searching." He writes:

> The effect [of the tale of the "panic-terror" of 1000 A.D.] may be rather like a good Halloween story. If told with relish, even an audience that doesn't believe in ghosts may wonder a bit about some coming fright; a few will buy into the full terror package. In the process, books or magazine articles will be sold, the public will have another kind of sensation to distract them, and maybe some useful

chastening of modern pride and superficiality will occur.

But he insists:

whether or not we want or need a good scare, as we approach the year 2000 we should at least get the facts about the past right and be properly suspicious of those who try to dish up demonstrable nonsense....

If we want to be afraid of the year 2000 or 2001, fine, but let's not pretend it's because of a clear medieval precedent. If we choose to be scared, fine, but let's recognize that our medieval ancestors weren't.

*   *   *

CALLING ALL DEAD-HEADS!

"New Year's Eve 1999 is the target date to open Terrapin Station, a $60 million museum, amusement park, concert hall, research center and center of the Earth for fans of the Grateful Dead music group. Two sites are still under consideration in San Francisco for the 65,000-square-foot museum, but Grateful Dead bassist Phil Lesh hopes Terrapin Station will be ready for a reunion concert of surviving Dead members on that fateful New Year's Eve."

—*Indianapolis Star*, Jan 25, 1998

Uncle John's
HANDY GUIDE TO THE
END OF THE WORLD
Part III

*Here are the end-time prophesies
of three familiar religions.*

CHRISTIANITY

Background: A 2000-year-old religion based on the teachings of Jesus Christ, considered the Son of God.

Signs the End Is Near: According to Dr. Douglas Ottati, an eminent Christian scholar, signs of the end are "very diverse...and can be very deceptive. One question that has to be answered," he says, "is: how dependable are they in the first place? Jesus Himself is often interpreted as having said that they're not very dependable." But not everyone agrees with that view; a number of events are regarded by many contemporary Christians as signs, based on *Revelation* and other parts of the Bible. For example:

• *The return of Jews to Israel.* Many consider the existence of the modern state of Israel to be a sign of the impending apocalypse.

• *The rise of China. Revelation* says an army of 200 million people will attack Israel at Armageddon. According to some sources, that's the current size of the Chinese army.

• *Development of computer technology. Revelation* says that in the end times, only people with the mark of the beast will be able to buy and sell goods. Some people think this could refer to computer technology such as bar codes.

• *The European Economic Community.* Many believe that the Antichrist must emerge from a united Europe.

When the World Ends: After much turmoil and strife, Christ will return and reign for a thousand-year period of peace. The battle of Armageddon will occur, evil will be defeated, and Judgment Day will arrive (see page 2063).

JUDAISM

Background: A 6,000-year-old monotheistic religion based on the Talmud (Jewish Oral Law) and the Torah (Written Law)—the first 5 books of the Old Testament.

Signs the End Is Near: The Messiah arrives. According to Rabbi Chaim Richman, this will be obvious, because "the world [will] be so drastically changed for the better that it [will] be absolutely incontestable!" For signs, he offers a list of "basic missions of the Messiah," including:

• "Cause the world to return to G-d and His teachings"

• "Oversee the rebuilding of Jerusalem, including the Temple, in the event that it has not yet been rebuilt."

• "Gather the Jewish people from all over the world and bring them home to the land of Israel."

When the World Ends: "Jews don't think in terms of the end of the world," says one scholar. "They think in terms of a new beginning. There's no cataclysm that marks this beginning. After the Messiah comes, people work in partnership with the Divine to bring about a better world."

ISLAM

Background: A religion founded in the 7th century by the prophet Muhammed. He experienced a series of divine visions which he wrote down in the *Koran*.

Signs the End Is Near: Mohammed Ali Ibn Zubair Ali says in *Signs of Qiyamah* that after the arrival of the Enlightened One, Imam Madhi, "the ground will cave in, fog or smoke will cover the skies for forty days. A night three nights long will follow the fog. After the night of three nights, the sun will rise in the west.The Beast from the earth will emerge. The Beast will talk to people and mark the faces of people. A breeze from the south causes sores in the armpits of Muslims which they will die from. The Qur'an will be lifted from the hearts of the people."

When the World Ends: "The Imam...will create a world state...He will teach you simple living and high thinking. With such a start he will establish an empire of God in this world. He will be the final demonstration and proof of God's merciful wish to acquaint man with the right ways of life."

Millennium Geography
WHERE DOES 2000 START?
Part II

*If you wanted to be the first person on earth to see
the dawn of the new millennium, where would
you go? That's what three island nations are
debating. (Part I is on page 2151.)*

I SLAND CONTENDERS
While officials in Greenwich insist that the year 2000
officially begins *there*, another debate rages halfway
around the world. Three South Pacific island nations
are fighting for millions of tourist dollars. Each wants to
be recognized as the first inhabited spot on the dateline
to see the new millennium. (The Antipodes Islands, an
uninhabited chain near the South Pole, will actually be
first.) The contenders are:

• **The Chatham Islands:** just east of New Zealand.
They aren't the closest to the dateline, but they're farther
south than the other two island countries and claim their
proximity to the South Pole will make them the first to
witness the sunrise.

• **Vava'u:** Part of the Tonga Islands. It's farther north
than the Chatham Islands, but physically lies closest to

2188

the dateline in its original form (as a straight line, without any bending).

• **The Republic of Kiribati:** An archipelago north of Tonga. It wasn't in the running until 1995, when its president moved a section of the dateline—which had previously split the country in two—tso it fit around its easternmost island, Caroline (changed to Millennium Island in 1997). Now the dateline at Kiribati juts farther east than at Vava'u. So they get the day's sun earlier.

DATELINE HISTORY

In case you're wondering how Kiribati could do that, here's the answer: The International Dateline was originally conceived at the 1884 Meridian Conference as a straight line running longitudinally from the North Pole to the South Pole. But immediately, countries complained that it cut through their island territories.

Russia, for example, wanted all of the Bering Strait included in the Russian day, so it asked that the dateline be curved 10 degrees to the east in that spot. The United States then asked for a reverse curve to the west to include the Aleutian Islands. The dateline was altered in both cases. In fact, to avoid such conflicts, the conference decided the line can be bent at will. Any government can redefine its time zone—and its place on the dateline—at any time. So although the move may be a little underhanded, Kirabati is within its rights.

TAKE YOUR PICK

Of course, not everyone recognizes Kiribati's dateline shift.

For example: A group of scientists writing in *The Geographical Journal* have definitively declared that Pitt Island, one of the Chatham Islands, will be the first inhabited island to see the sunrise. Why not Kiribati? "The arbitrary and unilateral moving of...the international dateline...lacks sensibility," they wrote.

However, it's been pointed out that one of the coauthors of the journal owns a business called the Millennium Adventure Company—which plans to film the sunrise from hilltops on Pitt Island. So that taints their argument.

The debate rages on: The Old Royal Observatory favors Pitt Island...but Dr. Roger Catchpole of the Royal Greenwich Observatory sides with Kiribati. "There are good administrative reasons why Kiribati put all of its islands on the same day," says Dr. Catchpole, adding: "Our calculations show that [the sun] rises there at 15:43 GMT, and that Pitt Island will see it around 16:00 GMT."

We're sure you haven't heard the end of this. By the way—on the other side of the dateline, Samoa will be the *last* place to see the start of the new millennium.

For More Info: greenwich2000.com/greenwich/meridian/ *or* www.goals.com/sailscin/dateline.htm

Jules Verne Hears the
"MUSIC OF THE FUTURE"

*In 1875, sci-fi great Jules Verne delivered a speech in
Amiens, France. It was presented as a dream he'd
had, in which he found himself wandering through the
city in the year 2000. We couldn't find a translation,
so we did our own. Here's a short passage.*

"On my left there arose a huge, hexagonal structure with a superb entrance-way....Posters plastered across the doors proclaimed, in gigantic letters:

PIANOWSKI
*Pianist of the Emperor
of the Sandwich Islands*

I was unfamiliar with both the emperor and his virtuoso.

"When did Pianowski get here?" I asked a fan, easily recognizable by his extraordinarily developed ears.

"He didn't get here," the native replied, looking at me with some surprise.

"So when's he coming?"

"He's not," came the fan's reply.

And this time, he seemed to be saying to

me, "Where did you come from?"

"But if he's not coming, when will he give his concert?"

"He's giving it now."

"Here?"

"Yes, here in Amiens, but at the same time, in London, Vienna, Rome, St. Petersburg, and Peking."

"Unbelievable!" I thought. "All these people are crazy! By any chance did they let the inmates out of the asylum?"

"Sir," I began again...

"But, Sir," the fan answered, shrugging his shoulders. "Read the poster! Don't you see that this is an electric concert?"

I read the poster! And indeed, at that very moment, the famous ivory-tickler Pianowski was playing in Paris, at the Hertz room; but by means of electric wires, his instrument was communicating with pianos in London, Vienna, Rome, Petersburg, and Peking.

Thus, when he struck a note, an identical note sounded on the keyboard of these distant pianos, whose every key was instantly moved by voltaic current!

Uncle John's
CELEBRITY PSYCHIC HOTLINE II

You've got questions…they've got answers. Of course, they could be the wrong answers…

HAL LINDSEY

Claim to Fame: Author of *The Late Great Planet Earth* and *Satan Is Alive and Well on Planet Earth*, two of the bestselling books of the 1970s. Both are full of apocalyptic Christian prophecies. They don't give any specific dates, but as one critic says, "Readers were left with little doubt that the end of the world was imminent—by the end of the eighties, at any rate."

Psychic Visions for 2000: In 1994, the earth was still alive and well, so he published updated versions of his prophecies in *Planet Earth 2000 A.D.* The plot: Russia joins forces with Islamic countries to invade Egypt and Israel. Europeans bomb the Russians, and 200 million Chinese cross the dried-up Euphrates River to attack the Europeans at Megiddo. Result: World war—leading to the battle of Armageddon and the second coming of Christ.

Believability Factor: If he was wrong about the 1970s and 1980s, why assume he's right about 2000?

Another consideration: Many of his original apocalyptic predictions relied on the existence of the Cold War and the Soviet Union. We don't have them to worry about any more…but Lindsey apparently isn't reassured.

And then, even after Lindsey "updates" his predictions, they can still wind up wrong. For example: In the early 1990s, he claimed that the 10-member European Economic Community was the "10-horned beast" that will appear before Christ's return. Since then, several new countries have joined. Maybe a few will drop out in time for the End…or maybe he'll "update" his predictions again.

POLLY THE COW

Claim to Fame: According to news reports, the Plainview, Minnesota cow predicted the winner of each presidential election from 1972 to 1988 "by relieving herself on a photograph of the eventual winner after equal numbers of the candidates' photographs were spread on the ground. The day before the 1992 election, after 10 photos each of Clinton, Bush, and Perot were spread out in a pen in a shopping mall parking lot, Polly's celebrated patty landed squarely on a photograph of Bill Clinton."

Psychic Visions for 2000: Unknown.

Believability Factor: Accurate or not, it's hard to think of a more appropriate way to predict the outcome of an election. Polly for president!

More Predictions from the Past
"IN 2000, WE WILL BE EATING..."

Don't like to eat fried mealworms and underwear? (See page 2004.) Maybe some of these other goodies will be more appetizing.

PETROLEUM AND POOP
"A number of companies, both here and abroad, are looking into the use of petroleum as a source of edible protein.

"Then, too, our space activities have led to a lot of food science research. What we're really after here is some means of processing human waste so as to return it into food channels."

—John Smith,
Science Digest (1967)

WATER FLEAS
"Man in [2000] may be eating 'water flea' steaks as a part of his daily diet [in 2000]. Dr. John R. Olive of Colorado State University said the 'water flea' Daphnia, is not really a flea at all but a bedbug-sized, soft-shelled crustacean that looks a

bit like a tiny clam. Preliminary experiments have shown that a water flea-algae mixture is palatable as soup either cooked or uncooked. The mixture can also be dehydrated into a paste or into dried cakes.

"'It has a taste somewhat similar to shrimp,' Dr. Olive said. With just a small amount of flavoring, the mixture can be made to taste like eggs or steak."

—*Science Digest,* (1961)

EDIBLE CANS

"[By 2000], you may dump the contents of a can of beans into the saucepan—and then chop up the can and toss it in, too. If it were a corn-flavored can, [you] could have a tasty bowl of succotash…an edible whipped-cream-flavored can to go with preserved strawberries…And a tomato ketchup-flavored container to surround canned baked beans should appeal to a wide public. "

—Norman V. Carlisle & Frank Latham,
Miracles Ahead! (1943)

Great Expectations
HEY—IT COULD HAPPEN!

As you might imagine, there are lots of big plans for the millennium that are still just plans. We're betting at least a few will fall by the wayside or mutate into something less impressive. Here are a few to keep track of.

THE MILLENNIUM DOME

The largest dome ever built. Located in Greenwich, England (just east of London), along the Greenwich meridian, it will hold 10,000 people and be electronically linked to other millennium sites in Britain. The interior will be divided into 12 zones (each with a different theme), spread throughout a central auditorium. One of the most ambitious features being planned: a giant replica of a person (gender unknown) sitting on the floor holding a giant baby. Visitors will be able to enter the figures, where they'll be treated to exhibitions on the body and views of the dome.

MILLENNIUM COUNTDOWN CLOCK

A colossal clock, formed by the 12 avenues that converge on the Parisian square known as Place Charles de Gaulle. The hour hand of the clock will be one of the avenues, lit up to 300 meters from the center. The minute hand will be another avenue, lit up to 500 meters with a different color. The second hand will be a laser beam that circles the city from the top of the Arc de Triomphe, which is at the center of the square. The countdown will climax at midnight with a light show and a party around the Arc de Triomphe.

BRITISH AIRWAYS MILLENNIUM WHEEL

Will be the world's biggest Ferris wheel, twice the height of the Statue of Liberty. The Wheel will hang over the River Thames in London, opposite Westminster, supported from just one side. It will largely be powered by the Thames. Purpose: "To provide the capital with a remarkable spectacle, millennium landmark and much-needed vantage point rolled into one."

TIMESPAN MONUMENT

A building that will sit on the Intercontinental Peace Bridge, spanning the International Dateline between the Diomedes Islands, a pair of islands that act as border markers between Russia and the U.S. Its intersecting walls will form a peak that points to the North Celestial Pole. Once in the building's atrium, visitors will be able to straddle the dateline (indicated on the floor), keeping a foot in two separate days, literally. Construction on the monument won't begin, however, until 2000 or 2001.

According to its creators, the monument is meant to "unite two islands, two countries, two continents, two days...it's a tangible expression of the search for peace."

EIFFEL TOWER EGG DROP

Just before midnight, according to *The Millennium Guide*, "a colossal egg will be delivered from the belly of the Tower...It will then hatch to reveal a bank of TV screens which will show footage of other millennium celebrations from across the globe. The egg-birth is to be accompanied by 2000 drummers beating a 'millennial rhythm.' At precisely seven minutes before midnight, the entire area will be bathed in light so powerful it will appear to be day. After midnight, the party will continue, and the egg will be used to send and receive friendly e-mails to and from other countries." STOP THE PRESSES—This one has already been cancelled.

THE WORLD'S LARGEST IGLOO

The Ice Hotel in Swedish Lapland will host a cold but unique millennium party. An ice-bar will dispense vodka to revellers. Arctic party-goers will sleep in heavy-duty sleeping bags on beds chiseled from solid ice. (The hotel is regularly built during autumn and melts the following spring.)

Uncle John's
HANDY GUIDE TO THE PROPHETS OF DOOM #4

You just can't get away from Nostradamus. On page 2101, we gave you a quick glimpse of his life and influence. Now he's back...as a Prophet of Doom.

N OSTRADAMUS (1503–1566)

Background: "He is," according James Finn Garner in *Apocalypse Wow!*, "the most famous, the most quoted, the most widely analyzed and apparently the most successful prophet in modern history."

Thousands of "experts" have produced interpretations of the cryptic quatrains in his 16th-century book *Centuries*, to show that he anticipated all the major events in Western history. He's credited with correctly predicting the reigns of Napolean and Hitler, the assassinations of the Kennedy brothers, even the rise of Saddam Hussein.

Doomsday 2000: Naturally, Nostradamus also had a vision of the end of the world. In what is possibly his most famous passage—Quatrain 72 of "Century 10"—he foresees nations at war, the world in upheaval, and the appearance of a "great king of terror." Unlike his other quatrains, this one specifies a date for our imminent demise:

The year 1999, seventh month,
A great king of terror will descend from the
    skies,
To resuscitate the great king of Angolmois,
Around this time Mars will reign for the good
    cause

There are plenty of "expert" interpretations of this quatrain...and as you might guess, none of them are particularly cheery. For example:

• In *The Prophecies of Nostradamus*, Erika Cheetha concludes: "Nostradamus seems to foresee the end of the world at the Millennium, the year 2000...[But] first we must suffer the Asian antichrist, 'the King of the Mongols'."

• In *The Complete Prophecies of Nostradamus*, Henry C. Roberts says that "a tremendous world revolution is foretold to take place in the year 1999, with a complete upheaval of existing social orders, preceded by world-wide wars."

• In *Doomsday: 1999 A.D.*, Charles Berlitz warns of "the possibility of the earth being struck by a gigantic heavenly body" which he believes could refer to a comet, planetoid, or giant meteor.

Believability Factor: Presumably, the only reason you'd take Nostradamus seriously is if you believed his other predictions. Here are a few of his quatrains, selected at random, along with a contemporary analysis. See what you think.

Quatrain: The great man will be struck down in the day by a thunderbolt / The evil deed predicted by the bearer of a petition / According to the prediction another falls at night time / Conflict in Reims, London, and pestilence in Tuscany.

Analysis: In *Nostradamus & the Millennium*, John Hogue cites this quatrain as a prediction of John and Robert Kennedy's assassinations. He says the first line is a reference to JFK; the second line refers to psychic Jeanne Dixon's attempt to forewarn JFK (!); the third to Robert Kennedy; and the fourth to events going on at the time of RFK's death.

Got that? Let's try another.

Quatrain: Liberty will not be recovered / A bold, black, base-born iniquitous man will occupy it / When the material of the bridge is completed / The Republic of Venice will be annoyed by Hister.

Analysis: In *Prophecies on World Events by Nostradamus*, Stewart Robb says that although Hister is an ancient Latin term for the Danube River, it is also an anagram for the name *Hitler* (one letter change is permitted with anagrams). So it refers to a bridge across the Danube that the Nazis built in 1941. Shortly after, he says, Nazis began infiltrating Italy—the "Republic of Venice."

About the Hister-Hitler Connection: During World War II, some scholars theorized that Hister is a misspelling of Hitler and suggested Nostradamus intentionally scrambled it to avoid trouble. But as one critic asks: "Why hide the name of a man who didn't even exist yet?"

ON THE OTHER HAND...

The Book of Predictions says Nostradamus gave a surprisingly detailed prediction of the rise and fall of Napoleon. They say he foretold of "an Emperor born near Italy" named "Pau. nay. loron"—an anagram for *Napaulon Roy*—who "for 14 years will rule with absolute power." (Napoleon did.)

The last of the Napoleon quatrains quoted in the book goes: "The captive prince, conquered, to Elba / He will pass the Gulf of Genoa by sea to Marseilles / He is completely conquered by a great effort of foreign forces...Will end his life far from where he was born / Among 5,000 people of strange customs and language / On a chalky island in the sea." Pretty amazing, huh?

Like a lot of these prophets, there seems to be enough accurate material to make what Nostradamus says intriguing. But in this case, we'll know for sure if he knew what he was talking about. Just watch the skies in July, 1999.

Jules Verne Visits...

AN AGRICULTURAL FAIR IN 2000 A.D.

Here's another excerpt from Jules Verne's dream about waking up in the year 2000. (The first excerpt is on page 2191.) It was translated for us from the original French by Alyson Waters.

"On all sides there were machines that had come from America, carried to the farthest extremes of progress. A live pig was put into one machine, and out came two hams.

Into another machine was placed a wriggling rabbit, and out came a fur hat with a perspiration-absorbent lining! This machine could swallow ordinary fleece and spit out a complete outfit made of fine cloth!

The other machine could devour a three-year-old calf and in exchange offer up both a piping-hot blanquette of veal and a pair of shiny ankle boots, etc.

But I could not stop to contemplate the miracles of human genius....I arrived at the stadium that was already groaning under the weight of all the important people.

A prize had just been given to the fattest man—just like in America in any self-respecting contest. The winner was so worthy of the prize that he had to be carried off with a crane.

After the fat-man contest came the skinny-woman contest…[and] next it was the babies' turn. There were several hundred of them, and prizes were awarded to the fattest, the youngest, and perhaps the one who cried the loudest. In fact, they were all obviously dying of thirst, and they were asking to drink in their own, entirely disagreeable way.

"Good Lord!," I said. "There will never be enough wet-nurses to...!"

A whistle interrupted me.

"What's happening?" I asked.

"It's the suckling machine," my doctor answered. "Stronger than 500 women from Normandy! You know, since the (rules against) celibacy, it was necessary to invent steam-powered suckling."

The three hundred babies had disappeared, their deafening cries followed by divine silence.

2205

Important Influence #6
THE JETSONS

Great philosophers, scientists, and sociologists
have shaped our expectations of the year 2000.
But in most cases, their influence pales in
comparison to the impact of the Jetsons.

CLAIM TO FAME They defined the year 2000 for millions of American kids. "For two generations," says one critic, "a mention of the year 2000 [has] conjured up images of a George Jetson-like existence, complete with robots and spacecars."

"The Jetsons'...vision of the future," notes The *Chicago Tribune*, "is permanently imprinted on the collective mind of the [Baby Boom] generation."

BACKGROUND In 1962, animators William Hanna and Joseph Barbera created a spinoff of their prime-time stone-age cartoon "The Flintstones."

But instead of transposing contemporary American society into the prehistoric past again, they projected it into the 21st century. "We went in the other direction—to space," Barbera recalls. "The space race was on everybody's mind in the sixties, and we thought we could have some fun and spoof the future at the same time." "The Jetsons" debuted in prime time on ABC-TV, September 23, 1962.

IMPACT THEN It originally aired at 7:30 p.m. on Sunday night—traditionally a kids' time slot. But against "Walt Disney's Wonderful World of Color" (NBC) and "Dennis the Menace" (CBS), it flopped. "The Jetsons" was cancelled after one season; only 24 episodes were filmed.

Nonetheless, America's vision of 2000 A.D. immediately expanded to include the futuristic gadgets Hanna-Barbera invented for the show: the Skypad Apartments (which were "raised and lowered on hydraulic lifts to stay clear of bad weather"), George's atomic-powered bubble, Rosie the Robot, a seeing-eye vacuum cleaner, a videophone, etc.

The Jetsons Return. The following year (1963), ABC scheduled "Jetsons" reruns as a regular Saturday morning cartoon show—and this time, the show did so well that it stayed there. For most of the next 20 years, the same 24 episodes ran over and over again on Saturdays.

The result: Practically every American born after 1950 saw (and was influenced by) them. In 1995, one writer for the *Columbus Dispatch* noted, "As a small boy, I remember figuring out that I would be 42 in the year 2000...I was quite confident I'd be living like George Jetson. I might even retire to the moon."

IMPACT NOW "The Jetsons" is still being shown on TV. In 1985, Hanna-Barbera created 41 new episodes for syndication (total: 65), and in 1990, the Jetsons had their own (not very good) feature film. "Their popularity really amazes," said Barbera in 1989. "It keeps getting stronger and stronger."

The standard. "The Jetsons" is still a standard that defines the year 2000 for many of us—even if we use it now to show how far we *haven't* come. For example:

- "The year 2000 is not going to be about spaceships or the Jetsons. The changes will come from science, medicine, and microchips. But our lifestyles will be basically the same." —*Chicago Tribune*

- "Despite all the grand predictions that we'd be soaring around town like George Jetson by now, air cars just don't seem to be in our future." —*Greensboro News and Record*

- "Forget George Jetson's spacemobile and the shiny steel spires of Metropolis. When the 21st century arrives, cars will still have wheels and buildings will still be made of concrete." —*Washington Post*

- "Where 25 years ago [futurists] might have envisioned a world akin to that of the Jetsons…today they are thinking and talking in more conventional terms." —*New York Times*

To Visit "The Jetsons": www.cybercomm.nl/~ivo/

Let the Sun Shine In
THE AGE OF AQUARIUS

Remember the song "The Age of Aquarius," from the musical Hair? It was one of the biggest hits of the 1960s... and helped spread the notion that an era of peace and love would begin in 2000. Here's an update.

BACKGROUND

The Zodiac is made up of a "ring" of 12 constellations. They mark the path through which the sun, moon and planets appear to travel in the sky.

In astrology, an "age" occurs when one of these constellations is located in the spot where the sun rises on the morning of March 21 (the spring equinox).

The constellation remains there for approximately 2,150 years. Then the constellation immediately preceding it on the Zodiac moves into that space. This is called the "precession of the equinoxes."

OK. SO WHAT AGE IS IT?

Most astrologers think we're currently in the last stages of the Age of Pisces and are about to begin the Age of Aquarius. That's good news—traditionally, the Zodiac sign of an age is also the pre-eminent influence on people's lives. Aquarius is usually associated with idealism, creative expression, humanitarianism, and equality. So astrologers expect an era of "harmony and understanding."

When does it start? For several decades, astrology buffs have indicated that 2000 would be the beginning of this wonderful new age. But it turns out the Age of Aquarius may not arrive in 2000...or 2010...or even 2100. In fact, the shift from one age to the next is so gradual that *no one* knows exactly when it will start. Most estimates range from about 2040 to 2300. But it could even be longer: James Sweitzer, of the Adler Planetarium, believes the shift will occur closer to 2700 A.D.

THE AQUARIAN AGE

How does this affect things? Not at all, say some astrologers. They feel an Aquarian change in the air anyway:

> The Age of Aquarius will not take place until 2040...Yet, why do I sense that we have already entered it?...The global use of electricity, the car, phone, television...invention of technology to shrink the globe with computers...These are all related to Aquarius. Perhaps we are already feeling its influence!
>
> —**Unidentified astrologer on the Internet**

Let the sun shine in.

Trivia 2000
MILLENNIANA

Here's even more useless information.

GLOBAL 2000: Why are so many countries observing the year 2000? As English is the international language of business, the Gregorian calendar is the international civil calendar. It may not be a holiday for all cultures, but everyone's going to join the party.

WEIRDEST PROPHET FOR 2000? That might be R. Flash Kingsley, who wrote *Inner State 2000 A.D.*, a book that attempts to predict the future by decoding road signs from the U.S. Interstate highway system. "Buckle up!" he declares in the introduction. "This book is a 21st-century driver's manual and planetary guide to the universe. Fasten your seat belt and steer into the cosmos."

IT'S A HIT! Prince may have written the definitive bi-millennial hit song, but not the first. In 1924, vaudevillian Al Bernard cut a novelty tune called "In Nineteen-Ninety-Nine" for the Edison record label. Sample lyrics:

In 1999, in 1999,
Although today we ride in style,
They'll look back on us and smile.
In 1999, it surely will be fine,
We'll have a lady president in 1999.

Our Favorite Prophet
THE AMERICAN NOSTRADAMUS

John Elfreth Watkins, Jr. has been called the "forgotten genius of forecasting" and "the Seer of the Century." Here's why.

BACKGROUND In 1900, *Ladies' Home Journal* invited journalist John Elfreth Watkins, Jr. to write an article for their December issue. Its title: "What May Happen in the Next Hundred Years."

"It was just one of many forecasts that appeared in the final months of the 19th century—with one crucial difference," says a critic. "Unlike his contemporaries, Watkins made predictions that turned out to be stunningly accurate."

To appreciate Watkins's achievement, remember what was going on in 1900: Production on primitive autos had just begun, but they were still just a novelty. Many people lived in squalor and ill health and died young. There was no such thing as an airplane. The first feature movie hadn't been made. The telephone had been invented a scant 25 years earlier. It was a whole different world at the turn of the last century, yet somehow Watkins described many details that would become true at the end of this one.

"These prophecies," he wrote in his introduction, "will seem strange, almost impossible." Some excerpts from his article:

• **"The American will be taller by from one to two inches.** His increase in stature will result from better health, due to vast reforms in medicine, sanitation, food and athletics. He will live fifty years instead of thirty-five as at present—for he will reside in the suburbs."

• **"Hot and cold air from spigots.** Hot or cold air will be turned on from spigots to regulate the temperature of a house as we now turn on hot or cold water from spigots to regulate the temperature of the bath....Rising early to build the furnace fire will be a task of the olden times. Homes will have no chimneys, because no smoke will be created within their walls."

• **"Ready-cooked meals will be bought from establishments similar to our bakeries of today.** Such wholesale cookery will be done in electric laboratories...equipped with electric stoves, and all sorts of electric devices, such as coffee-grinders, egg-beaters, stirrers, shakers, parers, meat-choppers, meat-saws, potato-mashers, lemon-squeezers, dishwashers, dish-dryers and the like. All such utensils will be washed in chemicals fatal to disease microbes."

- **"Photographs will be telegraphed from any distance.** If there be a battle in China a hundred years hence snapshots of its most striking events will be published in the newspapers an hour later. Even today photographs are being telegraphed over short distances. Photographs will reproduce all of Nature's colors."

- **"Automobiles will be cheaper than horses are today.** Farmers will own automobile hay-wagons, plows, harrows and hay-rakes. A one-pound motor in one of these vehicles will do the work of a pair of horses or more. Automobiles will have been substituted for every horse vehicle now known....The horse in harness will be as scarce, if, indeed, not scarcer, then as the yoked ox is today."

- **"Everybody will walk ten miles.** Gymnastics will begin in the nursery, where toys and games will be designed to strengthen the muscles. Exercise will be compulsory in the schools. Every school, college and community will have a complete gymnasium....A man or woman unable to walk ten miles at a stretch will be regarded as a weakling."

- **"Submarine boats submerged for days** will be capable of wiping a whole navy off the face of the deep."

- **"Telephones around the world.** Wireless telephone and telegraph circuits will span the world. A husband in the middle of the Atlantic will be able to converse with his wife sitting in her boudoir in Chicago. We will be able to telephone to China quite as readily as we now talk from New York to Brooklyn. By an automatic signal they will connect with any circuit in their locality without the intervention of a 'hello girl.'"

• **"Oranges...in Philadelphia.** Fast-flying refrigerators on land and sea will bring delicious fruits from the tropics and southern temperate zone within a few days. The farmer of South America, South Africa, Australia and the South Sea Islands, whose seasons are directly opposite to ours, will thus supply us in winter with fresh summer foods which cannot be grown here. Scientists will have discovered how to raise here many fruits now confined to much hotter or colder climates."

• **"Man will see around the world.** Persons and things of all kinds will be brought within focus of cameras connected electrically with screens at opposite ends of circuits, thousands of miles at a span. American audiences in their theatres will view upon huge curtains before them the coronations of kings in Europe or the progress of battles in the Orient....Thus the guns of a distant battle will be heard to boom when seen to blaze, and thus the lips of a remote actor or singer will be heard to utter words or music when seen to move."

RANDOM THOUGHTS...

I Give Up!

"From the failure of my...efforts to persuade the general public that the century ends on December 31, 2000, I have concluded that people simply don't want to believe it. They want the century to end on December 31, 1999. They want to get it over with....It's as if they believed a new millennium will bring a better world. Or maybe it's just that they can't wait for the big blow-off."

—Jack Smith,
Los Angeles Times

Something To Live For

"I know I'm going to live into the year 2000 and I know I'm going to see the Red Sox win a world championship. That's the only thing I've got left."

—Former Boston Red Sox
shortstop Johnny Pesky, 1989

Millennium Madness

"The millennium exerts a strange mystical pull on the human imagination. It affects people the way moonlight affects werewolves, the way sirens affect dogs."

—Peter Carlson,
Washington Post

Tune In, Turn On, Boot Up
"By the year 2000, pure information will be cheaper than water or electricity."

—Timothy Leary,
Chaos and Cyberculture, (1995)

Red, Brown, and Blue
"America's going to keep changing, [and] the great Hispanic immigration into the U.S. is changing us more than anything. By the year 2000 we will certainly be a lot less German, Irish and English and a lot more Spanish. Love it or hate it, but get used to it, amigo."

—Andy Rooney, 1995

Another Deadline?
"The year 2000 is creeping up; what happens when it's finally December 31, 1999, and you still aren't president of the company/rich/married/thin/a mother/extremely well adjusted? Are you honestly going to be able to tell yourself that the next century will be the one when you get serious?"

—Gail Collins, *Working Woman*, (1992)

Nutrition News
"In the year 2000, Twinkies from 1973 will still be fresh."

—Conan O'Brien, 1996

Have we crashed yet?
THE COMPUTER BUG
Part 3

Thinking about becoming a survivalist to protect yourself against the effects of Y2K? You could move to the hills, take yourself off the power grid, stock up on food and buy gold. Or you can be a little more optimistic and stay home. If you do, here's what you can do about...

YOUR COMPUTERS

Test your equipment. Set the date of your system to 11:55 p.m. December 31, 1999. Let the date roll over and see what happens. If something fails, you'll need to take action. Depending on the size of your business (or how many computers you have at home), you can either replace your system or hire programmers to rewrite the code. (Some companies advise against testing equipment yourself since some of your software may get damaged. Instead, they suggest you contact the manufacturer.)

Have standby equipment. Today's desktop and laptop computers are far more powerful than older machines. They also recognize that years have four, not two, digits. Start operating and storing vital information on newer equipment.

YOUR LIFE

Keep a paper trail. Have bank balances, credit card statements, utility bills, receipts and any other important records stored on both floppy disks *and* on paper.

Watch your money. Ask your banks and other financial institutions about their Y2K compliance. Call an accountant for advice or referrals. Also think about how Y2K will impact your investments (for better or worse). Keep some cash or traveler's checks on hand in case ATMs temporarily shut down.

Check your utilities. Find out if your local telephone, water, gas, and electric companies are "Y2K compliant"

Check your medications. Make sure your prescriptions are filled before 2000.

Prepare with your community: Connect with people to share information and ideas. Organize a neighborhood association and create backup plans together. Contact your Chamber of Commerce. Go to conferences (For a list of conferences start at www.y2kactionday.com/audiofiles/yardeni/global/global.ram).

Stay informed: Keep an eye out for magazine articles, visit websites, find out how local government agencies are coping with the problem (inquire about their plans and the costs involved) and contact a local or regional task force.

STAY UP-TO-DATE
Here's a brief list of Y2K websites:
- www.rv-Y2K.org
- www.hp.com/year2000/
- www.ibm.com/year2000
- www.y2knews. com/whybuy/whybuy.htm
- www.xerox. com/year2000/
- millennia-bcs.com/prep.htm
- www.mindspring.com/~tedderryberry/Y2Kgen.htm
- www.y2kwomen.com/
- www.comlinks.com/
- www.itpolicy.gsa.gov/mks/yr2000/y2khome.htm
- y2kchaos.com/
- www.prepare4y2k.com/

*　　　*　　　*

WE'RE THE GREATEST!

"We have sanitation, surgery, drainage, plumbing—every product of science and accessory of luxury. It seems impossible to imagine an improvement on what we have."
　　　　　　—*Washington Post* editorial, January 1, 1901

"The achievements of the nineteenth century will grow to the last syllable of recorded time. Their imprint upon the history of man is indelible and shall be linked in the chains of eternity."
　　　　　　—Arthur Bird, *Looking Forward*, 1903

Dreams & Schemes

IT'S 2000—MAKE A WISH!

*Remember when you were a kid and people asked,
"If you could have any wish, what would it be?"
Curiously, a lot of grown-ups seem to have decided
that the year 2000 is the right time to make
those wishes come true. For example...*

PHILADELPHIA II

Proposed By: Mike Gravel, former U.S. senator from Alaska (1969–1981)

His Wish: The planet Earth should hold a convention on January 1, 2001 to elect a world government and adopt a world constitution. He believes this could "end the anarchy" between nations and deal with problems like pollution. The new constitution would emphasize basic human rights.

Comment: "The U.N. is not up to the job because it represents governments not people." He wants the convention to be called Philadelphia II, after the original U.S. Constitutional Convention.

YEAR 2000 ORCHESTRA

Proposed By: Mary-Jane Newborn, Cincinnati, Ohio

Her Wish: When the new millennium is ushered in, everyone on earth should be making music. "Several years ago," she explains, "it occurred to me that it would really be wonderful if symphony orchestras in different cities linked up and played the same music at the same time." Searching for an occasion of "sufficient magnitude" to stage her simultaneous musical event, she hit upon a date: January 1, 2001.

Comment: "I don't know [what song everyone should be playing] yet, but I feel that it will make itself known, will well from within the hearts of people everywhere and clearly be recognized as The Song."

ECONOMIC JUSTICE

Proposed By: Francis Arinze, a Nigerian Roman Catholic cardinal based at the Vatican

His Wish: Economic justice. When 2000 arrives, all rich countries should eliminate Third World foreign debt in 2000, as a gesture of reconciliation. He made the proposal in 1994 at a meeting of the world's cardinals; they had gathered to discuss how the Church should mark the millennium.

Comment: "The great nations should think of the foreign debt of the so-called Third World and try to cancel the debt that year...or at least reduce it drastically."

SPACE HUNT

Proposed By: The Light Year Consortium

Their Wish: More space travel. To encourage it, they proposed a "treasure hunt in space" to the English Millennium Commission. They would send 20 one-pound coins (equal to 2,000 pennies in English currency) to the moon and other places around the solar system. Prizes would be awarded to anyone who could return the coins to Earth.

Comment: "There will be no secret about where the coins are," explains a spokesperson, "the difficult part will be bringing them back."

UNITED RELIGIONS

Proposed By: William E. Swing, Episcopal Bishop of the Diocese of California

His Wish: At the 50th anniversary of the founding of the United Nations in 1995, he announced a plan for a similar organization called the "United Religions." The U.R. assembly would meet once or twice a year to "reverse the use of religion to justify war, hate, violence, aggression and intolerance." It would begin operation in the year 2000.

Comment: Swing admitted the interfaith assembly faced obstacles. "But I am committed to making this happen," he told The *San Francisco Chronicle*.

$ Cashing in on 2000 $
MILLENNIUM FILM FESTIVAL II

*Looking for at least one good film with "2000" in the title?
As far as we can tell, that's about all you'll find.*

JONAH—WHO WILL BE 25 IN THE YEAR 2000 (1976)

Plot: Swiss director Alain Tanner's bittersweet story of eight disillusioned 1960s revolutionaries trying to adjust to life in the 1970s. The reference to 2000 comes up in the friends' spontaneous song about one character's unborn son, Jonah:

In the year 2000, Jonah will be 25 / At 25, the century will disgorge him.

The whale of history will disgorge Jonah / Who will be 25 in the year 2000.

That's the time left to us / To help get him out, out of the mess.

Reviews: "Actually, a pretty good film."
      —Uncle John
"Mature, playful, and entertaining." *—Video Movie Guide*

DEATH RAY 2000 (1981) *Pilot for the TV series "A Man Called Sloane"*

Plot: Superspy T. R. Sloane is sent to find and recover the Dehydrator, "a device that sucks the moisture out of your body, leaving you a shriveled-up raisin (or maybe a prune)."

Review: "So clichéd and predictable that only the most diehard James Bond–imitation fans will be compelled to watch."
—*Creature Features*

EQUALIZER 2000 (1987)

Plot: "Another Road Warrior-style post-Holocaust picture (set in Alaska, which is now a desert). A military/industrial compound protects the precious commodity of oil (sound familiar?). One of the guarding group's officers is betrayed, so his son takes off for the 'wasteland.' There he's captured by rebels, and eventually leads an assault on the compound." —*Film Encyclopedia of Science Fiction*

Review: "Ripoff of the Mad Max genre....Wall-to-wall action unfolds in furious, ludicrous fashion."
—*Creature Features*

MADRID IN THE YEAR 2000 (1925)

Plot / Review: Early silent film from Spain. An exploitation classic—the "futuristic" scenes of Madrid with newly constructed waterways and ships gliding past the Royal Palace were apparently so ludicrous that audiences burst out laughing—even in 1925. But you won't get a chance to appreciate it—unfortunately, no prints have survived.

Join Now!
MILLENNIUM ORGANIZATIONS

There are many organizations with a "2000 connection." Here are a few.

The Billennium Education Foundation
www.billennium.com/f/index.html
Created to celebrate the past 2000 years and inspire achievements to make the world better in the next millennium. One major goal is to make education available for everyone on the planet.

Electronic Millennium Project members.aol.com/caleha2000/
Created as a celebration of the turning of the millennium and the freedom of communication through the internet. It's resources are provided "by the people, for the people."

Joined Against Millennium Madness members.xoom.com/wwwjamm/index.html
A worldwirde non-profit organization designed to fight against "millennium madness of all kind."

Light 2000 www.light2000.com/
A network using the millennium countdown as a vehicle for setting and attaining global goals and visions by 2000.

Light Shift 2000: Let's Turn On the Light of the World www.lightshift.com/
A synchronized universal meditation is planned to raise the consciousness of humanity.

Millennium Foundation of Canada www.millennia.org/
A non-profit society based in British Columbia which calls upon citizens of Canada and the world to exercise their rights and "make a will for the earth."

Millennium Society www.millenniumsociety.org/
Non-profit, non-political group founded in 1979. It's purpose is celebrate the world's common heritage using the year 2000 as a rallying point.

The MillenniumVault Project www.tmvp.com/
Project which plans to construct 1000 year time vaults to store curerent artifacts and artwork until the year 3000.

Third Millennium www.thirdmil.org/
A national (U.S.), non-partisan, non-profit organization run by young adults (18-34 years old). It conducts research, provides speakers for colleges and civic groups, and offers solutions t long-term problems facing the U.S.

World Action for the Millennium www.wam2000.org/
This organization's goal for January 1, 2000 is to have "[everyone] who can be reached by communications systems...linked together to receive...a 1-minute a message.'

Where It's At:
WEB SITES

*There are far too many web sites devoted to the
millennium for us to list here. Here are a
few we think are the best:*

Billennium www.billennium.com/home-frame.htm
Home of "The Official Celebration of the Year 2000™."
This site features a countdown clock, a chat room, historical info, a survey, and offers ways to get involved.

Everything 2000 www.everything2000.com/
The website to go to for info on the turn of the millennium. Includes sections on events, resources, news, movements, travel, organizations, and Y2K.

FAS Millennia Monitor www.fas.org/2000/index.html
A website devoted to monitoring "apocalyptically inspired groups or individuals [who] might use weapons of mass destruction...over the next five years or so."

Greenwich 2000 www.londonw1.com/index.html
A good site to go to for history of the Greenwich Meridian. Also has event listings, news, and travel info.

Millennium Institute www.igc.org/millennium/
Contains interesting projects and ideas—a great site for philosophical discussion of the millennium.

Millennium Society www.millenniumsociety.org/
Contains a monthly calendar of events, a newsletter,
press releases, and suggestions on ways to get involved .

Millenniumania www.futurecast.com/millenniumania/
A great site for millennium links and news listings.

Millennium321 www.millennium321.com/
An attractive site with a futuristic look. Contains profiles
of futurists, events, products, and an interactive section.

Talk 2000 humnet.humberc.on.ca/talk2000.htm
This site is a "global town meeting" were participants discuss the folklore, events, and meaning of the year 2000.

The Year 2000 Information Center www.year2000.com/
A great site for information on the Y2K problem. Contains articles, links, advice, perspectives, conference listings, and products. (For more Y2K links, see page 2220.)

Third Millennium Challenge www.millennium.nl/
Very cool site with the look of an early 80s video game.
Has all the requisite millennium info as well as a game
room (must be Java enabled) and a chat room.

Worldwide Observatory of the Year www.tour-eiffel.fr/
teiffel/an2000_uk/
An impressive site which offers a virtual tour of the Eiffel
Tower. Also includes a list of events, a forum, historical
info, futurology, and a picture gallery.

RECOMMENDED READING

*Here are some of our favorite
books on the year 2000.*

• Cetron, Marvin, and O'Toole, Thomas, *Encounters with the Future: A Forecast of Life into the 21st Century* (McGraw-Hill Book Company, 1982)

• Collins, Gail and Dan, *The Millennium Book* (Bantam, Doubleday, Dell, Publishing Group, 1991)

• Garner, James Finn, *Apocalypse Wow!* (Simon & Schuster, 1997)

• Gould, Stephen, *Questioning the Millennium* (Harmony Books 1997)

• McClure, Kevin, *The Fortean Times Book of the Millennium* (John Brown Publishing Ltd, 1996)

• Rosen, Stephen, *Future Facts* (Simon & Schuster, 1976)

• Schwartz, Hillel, *Century's End: An Orientation Manual Toward the Year 2000* (Doubleday, 1996)

• Stearns, Peter N., *Millennium III Century XXI* (Harper-Collins Publishers, 1996)

• Wallenchinsky, David, Wallace, Amy and Wallace, Irving, *The People's Almanac Presents The Book of Predictions* (Bantam, 1981)

VISIT
UNCLE JOHN'S
WEBSITE!

www.unclejohn.com

- Trade great stories
- Become a member of the Bathroom Readers' Institute
- Help write future editions
- Order additional BRI books
- Visit our "Throne Room"— a great place to read!

Go With the Flow!